# SECRET TRUTHS

# SECRET TRUTHS

CHANNELED BY
## VIRGINIA ESSENE

S.E.E. PUBLISHING COMPANY
SANTA CLARA, CALIFORNIA USA

Cover illustration: Christina Nelson
Design: Nelson & Toews Design

ISBN #0-937147-01-X
Library of Congress Catalog Card Number:
86-063051

Spiritual Education Endeavors
Publishing Company
1556 Halford Avenue, #288
Santa Clara, CA 95051
USA

# D E D I C A T I O N

This book is dedicated to God—the original Creator of all life in the many dimensions, planes, and realms of reality—and to those great Rays, angels, teachers, and guides who patiently lead us back into true remembrance of our spiritual identity and purpose as cosmic beings.

It is also dedicated to all the spiritual brothers and sisters on earth who desire to be Caretakers and Peacemakers of this planet, particularly those of ages 14 to 23. It is also dedicated to the parents of young adults who must provide the New Age nurturance these souls in residence need as a foundation for the coming Time of Radiance.

Thank you for being here and for your courageous perseverance in the name of Universal Law that requires us to demonstrate peace upon this presently misguided planet. Because of your commitment peace is possible.

May you be truly blessed by those gifts of God already given and those yet to come.

# ACKNOWLEDGMENTS

A special word of thanks is given to Marijke Hoefnagels, Louise Kinoshita, Ann Valentin, and John Willis for their part in the preparation of this book, and to the many Love Corps networkers for their support and encouragement during the process of bringing forth this second book.

Most particularly I wish to thank Ann Valentin for her constant caring and concern.

I have already dedicated this book to God and those great Rays who guide our lives and the future of this planet, seeking always the preservation of all life and peace without ceasing. Now I wish to acknowledge that without their support this book would never have been conceived or written.

To the Gold, Silver, Blue, and Scarlet Rays, I once more say, "Thank you ... may your efforts bring that pinnacle of peace every loving heart desires."

# F O R E W O R D

Since the completion of the New Teachings for an Awakening Humanity book, I have continued to channel, or to mentally receive, information about humanity's present plight, about probable earth changes, and about the call for peace and preservation of all life, from four sources: the Christ energy (the Gold Ray); the Silver Ray, one of the first two creations of God; the Blue Ray (Archangel Michael); and the Scarlet Ray (Archangel Gabriel).

All of these beings, in addition to many others in both the spiritual and angelic realms, are urgently concerned with earth's problems and wish to assist us in this Time of Awakening ... this Time of Peace.

They have asked that I particularly try to reach young adults from "teens to twenties" (even though the information is useful for all ages), because this soul group, especially, contains the seeds of the Golden Age and comes to establish the Time of Radiance upon the planet.

Because of the different thought patterns and communication styles of these four great beings, it has been an arduous task to organize the various channelings into a coherent, meaningful message. In order to do this I have seldom directly quoted the information but the reader may sense the different styles, even though their separate material has been interwoven wherever possible.

There are two direct channelings quoted where the information was self-contained and long enough that it could stand by itself. These come toward the end of the book and are clearly identified as delivered by the Silver Ray and The Christ (Gold Ray).

My prayer is that this synthesized style will afford readability and consistency which some shorter channeled materials lack. At the same time I alone must accept responsibility for any flaws of presentation. Due to the rapidity of consolidating and editing these different messages I ask you to call to my attention any errors you notice.

We are definitely in the Time of Awakening and the news for 1987 to the mid-90's is: **expect change.** Yet any information presented here is to be cross-checked within your own knowing so that you follow the appropriate action unique to your particular soul's pattern and contract. Most of all we are told that every moment has the potential for joy and peace.

To you youthful members of planet earth I hope this book will give you something of value to ponder, something which will lead to an attitude of commitment and the desire to create peace now and forevermore. I hope it will encourage you to become a peaceful individual and to take that model forth to make the world a peaceful place. When many truly peaceful people work together peace will come!

If you wish to know more about the Love Corps, read the New Teachings book or use the order form at the end of this book to be in contact with us.

Most of all, I hope the book's message will urge you to begin meditating, to be consistent in your efforts to know and serve God, and to be part of that vast spiritual alliance of light which offers aid to our planet during this Time of Awakening.

# TABLE OF CONTENTS

# NOTE TO READERS

In God all things are ONE, and beings who are close to the Creator think as "we," "us" and "ours"—not "I," "me" and "mine."

Therefore, when the higher energies are communicating with us, "we" is frequently used by them, even though one distinctive energy may be thinking and communicating. Be aware of this as you read, noting the rare use of I, and just shift from the feeling of one speaker to a sense of several or many—even to a groupness or togetherness that could represent billions of energies.

It is this change from one to many—from a place of I and me separation to a unifying wholeness of we and us—that humanity is called upon to demonstrate during this New Age.

# CHAPTER I
# WHY YOU CAME TO PLANET EARTH

And so it is time for you to know the truth about who you are and why you are living on the planet earth during this period of time called the 20th Century, A.D.

You chose to come and help rescue the planet. There are only a few adults on your planet who have learned the great secret teachings and can tell you these things. Perhaps you are a fortunate person who lives among adults of great knowing. All the better if you are. But if you are not, it is very important that you be told immediately about these coming years. This is because there likely will be great earth changes to be experienced in order that you might have a peaceful planet.

The purpose of these changes will be explained to you in this book, so that you will not be confused or unprepared for the things which will surely come if your peoples and your nations do not seek peace! The monstrous attitudes of war, violence and negative thinking, which are so prevalent on your planet at this time, must be reversed. These attitudes threaten to snuff out a majority of the life you now take for granted—not only the life of human beings but also the life of animals, birds, plants, trees, flowers, and every other living organism that creates the great web of interrelated life where you

1

are. These attitudes must change if life is to continue peacefully on planet earth!

You are one of millions of young adults on the planet, one of 30-40 million just in the United States alone—and time is short! This book is for you and those like you who are ready to remember your true origins and your life's purpose as a Caretaker of planet earth.

Then let us begin at the beginning, before life as you know it existed on this planet earth, and share what the truth of your soul is.

Over eight million years ago, you were a light body similar to that of beings you call angels. Your body weight and structure were very different then, and you had only a few of the physical characteristics that you know as "normal" today. Let us say you were glowing with a beautiful light, that you had an outline similar in design to what you have now. Remember, you are not just the physical body which you see reflected in mirrors and which appears to be the great certainty of your existence. No, you are still that light, that glowing brilliance encased or temporarily residing in your physical body. Yes, now you have taken on the physicalness of earth, to be able to stay in what is called a third-dimensional world, for learning and service. You are learning to love and care for God and for all of life in its various forms.

Actually, your source of this light and energy—something like electricity, if you can imagine that—has a homeland far from this one, which you are capable of visiting sometimes during sleep. And you and all life energy were created by what you call God.

Who or what are you? YOU ARE LIGHT AND ENERGY! When something happens to your body or "earth suit," your higher and more knowledgeable self returns to its higher life, or dimensions, or activities, to that world your holy books have called "heaven."

Heaven is merely a general word that lumps together the places where life continues after that experience called "death." And, in a way, you died when you left your magnificent eternal homeland, heaven, and entered this phase of learning experience or school called earth. Here it is nearly impossible to remember what we are speaking of, but be assured, your life will continue when you exit from this "Earth School," even as you lived before visiting this planet.

Can you grasp a little bit of what we are saying? When that great ONE called God, Source, or Force created you of Itself, your nature was light and energy. When this life giving energy burst forth into its two aspects—the gold and silver rays—trillions and trillions of energy particles were later created by them, which eventually expanded into twelve holy light Universes. These worlds beyond counting cradled multiple lifeforms and planets, stars, star clusters, galaxies, novas, and glowing suns and much more that is spoken of in your field of astronomy. The reality of all this is far greater than we can briefly describe or than you can see when you look up at the night sky. But by watching the night sky some of the sparkling proof of what we have mentioned may arouse your soul's recollection about your origin and purpose on earth.

More, even, than the flowers that bloom, than the sand on the beaches, or the drops of water in the oceans—more than all this is the magnificent, ever-growing family of God, scattered far beyond your ability to count or measure. It is too vast for you to experience presently and yet it is all related by the common heritage of energy and light that created it.

Know, then, that a spark of the Divine or unlimited Creator resides in you, even though you left your higher life to visit the planet earth for additional schooling and service.

3

Now, you may be wondering, "Why would I leave my homeland to come to earth?" This is a logical question. Let it be answered this way. Whenever a new planet is made ready for life of any kind, including that which you call human, those of the spiritual eternal flame quality are asked if they would like to have an adventure in growth and learning. And those who volunteer, who are appraised to be suitable and who pledge to complete their mission, are given the opportunity to join others on the new planet which needs Caretakers to oversee the unfolding of life in all its expressions. You came to earth as one of the Caretakers of its life eight million years ago. **Then you did not have a dense physical body as you have now.**

Like a great armada, those spiritualized energies came to earth, together constituting the spiritual family of Caretakers to complete the task they had chosen. All was in readiness for a great adventure. Those millions of glowing, non-physical souls were excited and challenged by their new environment and, above the planet's surface they discovered, learned, and cared for the life they found. They were wonderfully happy and lived in their light bodies for many thousands of years.

In fact, for nearly a million years life was truly enjoyable. And then a great change occurred.

In their original agreement to come to earth, the light beings had promised that, no matter what happened, they would always remember their Creator with love and reverence, and would always stay true to the purpose of preservation of all life on the planet.

The planet was created as an experiment in free will, so you live on a FREE WILL planet. (Free will means each soul can choose whatever it wishes to do.) Since only positive energy had been present for a million years, there was nothing of negativity to unbalance this beautiful free will creation. But then negativity was allowed to enter the planetary area, so a true free will situation would exist. And that, Children of the Light, is where the trouble began.

Ever since they had left their homelands behind, these spiritual pioneers still maintained communication with their former existence by means of what you might call mental telepathy. It was a lifeline to those former homelands and enabled them to receive guidance about problems, difficulties, or concerns they were having. It was similar to a two-way radio, walkie-talkie set or mental TV. You can understand that this communication link was vital for those on this spiritual outpost in a far corner of the Universe.

Since the purpose of coming to earth as a Caretaker was to learn to love God through every difficulty and not to abandon belief in the Parent which had created it, each soul was now put to a crucial test as part of its learning experience—something like an examination in a school course.

Up until this moment on the planet, the beings of light were all peace and harmony. They cared for all lifeforms who needed assistance, aided one another if help was necessary, and lived a glorious life of beauty and serenity. Their minds were connected both to one another and to God. And because of this communication, life proceeded naturally as had been planned.

Then the challenge came.

Only a few of your earth books speak of that time of darkness or separation in true perspective which is why you are being given this information now. Many of your teachings do say there came a deep sleep, a separation, or a falling away from the God who had created them. But most teachings fail to explain that you had volunteered to come to the planet to learn self-mastery as love-beings. They do not tell you that the time in which you live today is the final time, the end of that great

eight million year period you began so long ago. It is the clo-
sure of many cycles; it is the time of graduation.

When the power of negative thinking began on earth, many
of the light beings began to get involved with and in the lifeforms which they were supposedly caring for, and there was an
intermingling of their light with the grossness of the lesser,
material world. This has been called temptation by some holy
books. The temptation to go off and do whatever the individual soul chose to do prevailed, and the messages of support and
warning that still could be heard within the mind as if by radio
or TV were ignored. Thus the lowering of sound and light vibrations continued for eons, until many were no longer capable
of hearing the God voice within.

Much of this happened after a negative, unloving power
came to encourage the light people to ignore what they had
agreed to do. This dark influence over the formerly loving
Caretakers continued for millions of years, with only a mi-
nority of the people able to remember God, to hear constructive
guidance on that inner home telephone. And, although there
were many "rescue teams" sent to remind the light beings, now
fallen, of their need to return to their original agreements, if
they were to have self-mastery and receive what you might call
a promotion into higher cosmic activities, none had much real
effect.

Now you are here—eight million years later—with one last
opportunity in that asked-for self-mastery course you undertook. While there is still time to re-establish peace on earth,
you are challenged to preserve all life and to revere and remember God, that great ONE from which all life sprang.

So that is the setting in which your own personal life now
exists. And the questions we ask you to consider are: Do you
wish to remember why you came to earth long ago? Will you
join your efforts with millions of others like yourself who are

just now awakening?—just now ready to pick up the torch of certainty and commitment and move into a graduation of your soul's planetary initiation? You live on the earth, but this is not your primary heritage. It is a step, a stage, part of a vast learning process from which you may be promoted to even greater opportunities. Or you can be the foundation of a great new civilization of heaven on earth, if you wish. The world needs peace! Will you bring that message and be its model?

There will be those who insist, "Prove what you say" or "How can I know this is the truth?" Our reply to this doubt would be that you listen with your heart. That is the one infallible tool humanity has possessed since its fall from that former ability to communicate with God. For your heart feels and remembers God. It is your soul connection to the Cosmos.

Today your only true guide is that spark of God within you that will direct your path and make your journey as easy as possible. This is the present plight of your fellow beings on the planet: they are asleep; they have forgotten; they are unconscious. But that unconsciousness must be ended if peace is to return to the planet and if you are to escape the ravages of a self-created nuclear war, the effects of underground explosions, Star Wars weaponry, or worse.

Your proof of any new information is the way you feel inside. For instance, if this message rings within you an inner bell of some kind, it is your truth. If not, you may find other helpful information or you may continue to sleep until one day, in some faraway place, you will again be given the chance to learn this commitment of caring through thick and thin, of loving God without ceasing.

Time means nothing to God. Only in these physical worlds does it exist, and time has a way of being interminable and exhausting. Let your heart remember your mission, then, and please use these remaining years to good benefit. Your task

7

can still be completed, whether you are an angel that forgot itself, a child of angels that forgot, a rescuer of angels that became entrapped here, or a soul which still prefers to do as it pleases regardless of the original earth agreement.

If you dare to remember your true inheritance, God's love corps welcomes you home again and seeks to bring about the completion of that adventure which you undertook so long ago. Jesus the Christ was one being who, along with others down through time, remembered fully and completely his true God-identity while living in a body. **Christ means light!** You are light remembering itself—its true self. And you have many great opportunities now to achieve the goal, set eight million years ago, before the earth was physically populated.

The present difficult circumstances on earth involve karmic law (or the principle of cause and effect), and it is consequently a time of intense challenge for the planet and all of humanity because of those returning negative effects that must now be faced.

During this time the call is going out to many like yourself; it is the call to work together in order to save planet earth from disaster. You will not be alone. You are needed! Can we count on you?

Humanity and the planet must be healed! All of you can help with this regardless of your age, size, color, or religion. Yes, this is the Time of Awakening. Will you receive God's love and energy and awaken to **your** true spiritual identity?

If, as a young person, you have not read of these things in your history books or if you have not gleaned them from the books you call the holy scriptures or from the teachings of a religion, do not be surprised. You are still one of the Caretakers of the earth, even if nearly everyone on this planet has forgotten what this means.

If you awaken now, perhaps you can help persuade your sleeping fellow humans to give up war, attack, and killing, and to model peace as an example to others. Humanity must learn to care for all of life with great intensity, whether it be the minerals, the animals, the plants and trees, or the birds and mammals of land and sea.

Being, then, a responsible person—whatever your age—you will recognize in your heart that the future of planet earth is partially in your hands. There are many who have totally forgotten their mission, who have forgotten who they are in the spiritual realms, who have aligned themselves with pursuits and interests which do not acknowledge the need for peace and the preservation of all life. Yet they can still awaken to their souls' and God's calling.

Then share the truth of who and what you are: *energy* (something like electricity or electromagnetic energy). Share that you have a common identity springing from that great ONE who is often called God. Share that in this relationship between you and God, or you and your creative source, the Parent-of-all, you have a purpose far beyond the little planet you live upon now. You have relationships in vast corners of this Universe and you have power and responsibilities at many other levels. You have the type of power that is creative in nature, if accompanied by a nurturing and caring attitude. Nothing here on earth has been created that is not cared about by the spiritual ones who assist you!

The very act of creating anything—whether a tree house, a toy, a picture, a song, a home or airplane of some kind—begins with a thought, a picture, a blueprint, or an idea seeking fulfillment. Even God's energy, in the creation of your planet, had an idea or concept to follow or you would not be here. For the idea contained the visualization of what would happen after it was finished. The expectation was that, over eons of time, the individual cellular, molecular, microbiological lifeforms would grow and expand and, one day, would create the basis of a simple pattern out of which much else would follow.

And in all of this planning there was peace and harmony, excitement and joy, and the interest to see how it would all work out eventually, so that each lifeform would be honored. For God is not limited by time. Time is only a measurement for you on earth to segregate and separate things and people, one from another. Since God knows no separation, there is, in truth, no time.

The most important thing for you as a young person to understand is that each little piece of life or creation is vital. All are part of a gigantic undertaking of wholeness and relationship called symbiosis. Symbiosis, or harmony in and through relationships, has its cycles and nothing remains static or changeless for long, except God and God's first creations.

This planet is not a duplicate of any other planet. It is unique. The thing that is unique or most unusual about it is that God's creative force wanted this planet to be one of *caring and peace,* although free will in nature. For not all planets are of this type. Since earth was set in motion to be both free will and a loving peaceful planet, you who live here cannot change that pattern—you can only demonstrate it. Its purpose is already defined, just as the purposes of the other planets in your solar system have been defined.

Then ponder what has been said. Close your eyes, shut the book and hold it in your lap a few minutes.

Be quiet for a while and listen within.

. . . . . . . . . . . . . . . . . . . . . . . . . . . . . . . . . . . . . . . . . . .

Only if you really feel drawn to continue reading this book should you do so. For some people are ready to remember and some are not.

Follow your inner knowing only, not the senseless monkey-mind chatter of the limited human personality which is an illusionary substitute for God's truth and peace.

Ask the God-spark within you what your course of action should be, for in spite of this long spiritual sleep, that spark can glow again and bring you back to God. It is an infallible map to buried treasures of spiritual gold and silver. It is your return ticket to Cosmic truth.

# CHAPTER II
# EVOLUTION OF THE HUMAN
# BODY AND THE PLANET EARTH

In the planning of the human body, over the evolutionary experience called "time," it was necessary to make constant adaptations in design, rather than one action of creating the body and then having no further changes. There have, in fact, been many models, even as you create improvements and changes in those things called automobiles and airplanes. Know also that changes are being made even now.

What you call the human body has been experimented with for 4.5 million years because, after losing its etheric form (like the angelic energy depicted in books), humanity needed a new, more solid or fleshy form. Therefore, the human physical body is merely a prototype, an example, an experiment, caused or created by God and specifically designed by the higher forces and Rays. Your parent, the Creator, has made many lifeforms in this and many other Universes, using a variety of designs. The size, shape and appearance of these lifeforms are usually based on specific elements such as oxygen, hydrogen, nitrogen, carbon or other complexities and compounds unknown on earth. Each is unique in some way, yet each is brought forth by the energy of God.

The human body you have now had to be tried out and is not the same body in which spiritual or soul residence was taken millions of years ago, nor even 50,000 years ago. There have been many adaptations made already, and more will be made through a process of genetic design and energy upgrading of the DNA, RNA, and other cellular structures and patterns of the body. Your scientists are just beginning to explore these with any clear understanding.

Because a full grown human being couldn't be created within another adult human being, there are stages of development and growth designed into your body which you had to go through in order to get from conception and birth to babyhood and gradually to adult size. This process is a truly miraculous creation, if you stop to think about it. Could you create such an intricate blueprint?

Yes, the body is a miracle. A creative miracle. It is a gift to you which must be cared for, so do not harm it. Neither your own nor another's! Maintain your light and love energy in it as long as you can—in a state or condition of peace. Peacefulness extends the life span of this particular vehicle called your body, for it was not built to be worn down with stress and excessive tensions such as those caused by hatred and violence or even misfeeding.

We would remind you that your diet and the ingestion of poisons, toxins, dyes and additives in food do not extend your body's life. Quite the contrary. Drugs, chemicals and toxins were not programmed into the nature of your body's metabolism. In fact, it was designed to feed upon vegetable and plant substances that had a vital life still in them, so an energy exchange could be made from one lifeform to another. Thus, nuts and seeds and fruits and that which you call vegetables and roots—even herbs—were the fuel which was expected to safely energize the body. These natural substances, alone, could allow a transfer of energy from one living thing to another. This is utilizing and fulfilling God's plan for fueling one living thing with another living substance. The plants were especially created to feed others and need to be thanked and appreciated for fulfilling God's purpose.

Living foods will energize your body. Non-living foods, or what you call "junk" food, will hurt the body over time and cause faster breakdown of various parts and functions. This generally means pain! If you allow your body structure to break down, it will hurt. Your body will be harmed even further if you allow doctors to treat the condition by burning and poisoning the body vehicle in an attempt to make its cells regenerate—to make it well again. When physicians revere the body creation as God's gift and follow a natural path of healing, including the living foods, technically-oriented humans will have better health. This is preventative, not reactionary, medicine.

Again, I remind you that you have a body designed by God and by profound thinkers and master designers. It is a true work of art. It was made to be self-healing and long lasting, but it has been abused on earth due to your modern technological existence and wears out quickly. Over eons of time as the planet is transformed and physical life rejuvenates you will notice improvements should you come back into a body again.

Like noticing an updated car, you will say, "They have certainly improved on this model!" We joke with you but also insist that your body is a truly wonderful life suit to have and that *you* are responsible for its care.

Let it be known to all young people from age 13 up that you are responsible for your body and you alone will bear the pain of its damage or injury due to accident or abuse. In future times we will be able to build in, or evolve, self-healing aspects such as regrowing limbs. These things may seem quite "far out" to you at the present, but they are coming for those of the *light* who serve God.

15

Much has been said about reverence and appreciation for the things of this planet, including your body form. This is urgent to remember! It grieves us to say that most people on this planet have not held the lifeforms of humans, animals, plants, or minerals in appreciation and caring. Some things will have to transpire upon this planet, therefore, to heal and cleanse the damage that humanity has caused at many levels. Not only will your body and all other lifeforms be affected, but the living planet will be cleansed, too.

Why?

Because the planet is a created living thing even as you are and has been abused by humanity. (We will say "she" hereafter because the purpose of the planet's creation is *nurturance* and that quality is commonly considered a feminine attribute in your thinking.) She also has a physical body, feelings or emotions, a mind and a spiritual nature. Although she is like her brother and sister planets in your solar system, she is still unique. Yet she must not hamper her solar family's evolutionary pattern. Truly she has her own path, her own God-given purpose to fulfill, even as you do. She is evolving, changing, becoming an example of love and peace though situated in a free will Universe where negativity abounds.

You are like a cell in her body and so what she must be and do will affect you and all life upon the planet. You need to understand that the way you and every other human person behaves either supports or detracts from her own needs and purpose. Would you really deny your homeland her galactic stardom? This is her hour of transformation just as it is yours.

Let us imagine the planet earth as a huge home or hotel with many rooms and different activities going on inside. Now if the majority of these rooms and activities are harmonious and useful, the home or hotel is well-known for its positiveness and enjoys a pleasant reputation. It earns a reputation for harmony and wholesome value. On your earth you speak of maintaining property values. Then know that your greatest responsibility is to maintain earth's property values, those qualities of life which are nurturing, peaceful, joyful, and ever growing in cosmic awareness.

Your small part of earth's greater identity is the basis for her growth in love and wisdom. Together you are a whole package in design. Earth and you are a unified identity, a team, a family growing richer in consciousness.

Your increased understanding of this principle is critical to you of earth at this time so we will review the concept this way. Your earth is part of a network of *100 billion galaxies* of different shapes and sizes called a UNIVERSE. So even your Milky Way galaxy home is part of a huge creation almost beyond description. Inside of the Milky Way galaxy you have many living creations of the First Cause, one of which is your small solar system. So your solar system also has an enormous family and that family has far flung relatives of light and energy farther than you can see even on a starry night. And when you look into the sky and see all that has been created, you soulfully know an immense life exists and that somehow you have a part in it.

This feeling of reverence, this acknowledgment of the Creator's handiwork, is health. Health is a spiritual attribute. Health begins in your soul which gives health to your mind and emotions and thence to your physical body. This feeling of reverence should permeate everything you do. It should be the basis for a purposeful relationship within yourself, within your human family and friends, and within the broader society called city, state, nation, and planet. Regretfully, humanity has become so irreverent and negative within planet earth's consciousness, that she has become known as the darkest planet in your solar system, and is not even allowed representation on the Supreme Solar Council.

We do not say this to make you feel despondent or guilty, nor to have you give up hope that all is lost. Rather, all of us come in peace to tell you that we are asking you to wake up to what you are doing so that it may be changed for the better! *You are important.* You are a powerful agent for change, not only in your own life, but in your local environment. You are important to your city and town, to your state, and to your individual country. But you are also important to the planet itself and all life upon it because you possess the God-given ability to change your ideas and actions. You have free will. You can choose to wake up to God's plan and purpose joyfully, with anticipation for its majestic gifts.

This is that time on earth for changing the negative to the positive. You are here as an individual soul with mighty vision. You were born with the power to give that greater vision a reality! In this you are a co-creator with God, even on this small place within a mighty Universe. God-glorification here on planet earth is only possible through your wisdom and love, else it does not exist. *You* are the vessel or channel of that power. *You* alone can bring the vision of peace to a dying civilization, rekindle awareness, and implement peace here. Do not let the lazy, uninformed, or misguided tell you it can't be done, for it can. But effort is required. Will you help humanity, yourself, and your planet, as we of the God-love call you forth and place our knowledge and assistance at your disposal?

An answer, "Yes!" followed with ongoing enthusiasm and commitment could help arouse this darkened humanity which harms and limits this garden planet in God's vast firmament. Time is critical. *You* are needed! Will you help? Please sit quietly for a while and consider what has been said.

. . . . . . . . . . . . . . . . . . . . . . . . . . . . . . . . . . . . . . . . . . . . . . .

Now, why is the cleansing of the planet itself necessary? Well, if your own house becomes horribly soiled and dirty, you have to get the grime out of it. Perhaps you use a broom to sweep or a vacuum cleaner to suck the dirt out. Maybe you wash windows, walls, floors, and fixtures. Sometimes there's a need to paint or to strip off old varnish, patch cement, and so forth. The worse you have allowed it to become, the harder or more difficult the task is of fixing it.

**This cleansing is, in effect, the next stage of evolution for humanity and the planet. It has become necessary only because humanity abandoned the original plan for peace.** This program of corrective action is needed in order for humanity to enter the Time of Radiance. It is truly a stepping stone to a future you are only now becoming conscious of.

Since the earth is the house of humanity, how then can you cleanse her of yesterday's debris, heal her from the direct injury of underground nuclear blasting, and the negative thoughts of war and hatred that encase her in the putrid smog of violence and noncaring? Since your planet is ill, poisoned by heartless humans in many ways, this clean-up time is necessary.

Now let us explain *your* part in influencing the severity or thoroughness of cleansing which the planet will require. You have choices about how difficult this time of cleansing will be on earth. For just as a house gets disordered and chaotic during cleaning or remodeling, so the planet may have to undergo similar processes in order to get well. Yes, planet earth is ill, diseased! And it is your role to help her get well, just as you would want any loved one to be healed. As we have said, you are a single cell or unit of planet earth's identity as a multi-level creation, and as you heal, so does she.

The amount and the kind of cleansing to be experienced upon the planet's surface lies in an area called **PROBABILITY** and is related not only to humanity's past behavior, but to *present* intention and positive actions.

This earth cleansing is based upon the "cause and effect" principle of the Universe which all life must follow. If you are caring, caring returns. If you do not show courtesy, thoughtfulness, and consideration for all life, whether toward your human brothers and sisters, the planet, or the galaxy, the reflection back from those negative attitudes may be extremely uncomfortable and painful. Since humanity is not loving and honoring its planetary homeland, this must change!

You are the peace*makers*, not the peace*takers*, and it is hoped that the majority of humanity will assume responsibility to demonstrate peace upon the earth, among themselves, and in all planetary activities. So let your various groups and nations decide to have peace and work in close concert to promote and create peace. *Know, absolutely, that you have the power to help make this planet a wonderful place on which to live!* By your example the light grows and expands and shines its glowing harmony to humans, to the planet, even to the Creator-of-All-Things. When many agree to be peaceful, and so behave, the many physical earth changes of cleansing may be less severe. But humanity must cease its weapons and military pursuits at once. By bombing the bowels of earth with your underground weapons testing programs you invite disaster and internal upheavals of many kinds. Would you allow internal explosions in your own body's guts? Then prohibit such government and military activities! To do less is suicidal.

By your major space weaponry you not only damage earth's physical body, but her emotional and mental bodies as well, for these exist above the planet's surface in layers of energy vibration or consciousness that are invisible to you. As we have said elsewhere, the dangers of your space weaponry testing go far beyond the limitations of your flesh and body, and the multiple levels of the planet's being, into the very fabric of creation.

Things which are likely to happen on earth while she tries to adjust these inner and outer pressures are: earthquakes, volcanic eruptions, tornadoes, hurricanes, floods, high winds, and unexpectedly bitter weather conditions. *Now, this is not said to frighten you!* For fear creates chaos, and chaos is not helpful! Focus instead on the fact that for all who assist God's forces in the creation of peace on the planet there is great inner guidance, protection, and support available in dreams, meditation, and by intuition. You can help stop these probabilities or lessen their intensity. Always see a yet greater vision and opportunity during this earth epoch!! FOCUS on this opportunity, then, and be contented. Focusing on the *positive effort* will be energizing for all and will achieve much. Even if some cleansing should occur, you will only experience that which you need for the highest learning for your soul. You can help those who allow fear to emotionally paralyze themselves by assisting them to face that fear and reach a healthy understanding of what is happening so they too may join this grand effort for peace. This period on your planet is a time of great learning and self-cleansing for all, young and old alike. This cleansing can be eased and assisted by your understanding, your willingness to persevere, and by your devotion to God.

What we want to do is support your caring intentions, bolster your attitude of love and purpose, and give you every opportunity to demonstrate your caring for God. It is exactly this type of human being which will survive the earth changes and then become the foundation for the new civilization that will emerge after the storms and changes.

After the Time of Awakening and of Reckoning comes the Time of Radiance, a golden time of peace, when all beings of goodwill can group together for the greater understanding and the comradeship that spiritual clarity brings. This will be a new world, a new time, and if it is your desire to have it so, then we enclose you in the safety of that peaceful commitment and accept your pledge to put your energy to God's use. In this you will find great satisfaction, joy, and harmony. Indeed, it could be a time of heaven on earth for those who make it so.

If your answer to the question, "Do you want peace?" is "Yes," then God's answer will be "Yes." For the energy reflected back will be in balance with that given. You must understand that on a free will planet such as earth, every person has the right to do what s/he wishes and no one is forced to love or appreciate God. Therefore, many will ignore this information and never answer "Yes" to the question, "Do you want peace?"

Some humans will move farther and farther away from God and will continue to dump hostility, war, and hatred on all they meet. It is their choice while here on earth and, unless their deeds really endanger the planet itself or the life-filled space beyond it, God may choose a role of non-interference. Humanity will be stopped from assaulting space, of course, and should treat others as they would be treated, else they will bring an unexpected, painful response for that disregard and hateful attitude back to themselves. None of the warriors and inhuman scientists will be allowed to remain on this place when peace finally comes to reign, however. Thus, the cleansing will affect not only the physical aspects of the planet and humankind but their spiritual, mental and emotional qualities as well.

Now, you can do little about another person's choice to ignore God and resist peace on your planet beyond just modeling peace and calling others forth to try it also. If they choose not to change there is nothing more expected of you. You merely proclaim the truth and live it. If others will not learn from your example and our spiritual proclamations and teachings, they will one day be sent back to a remedial opportunity where they can acquire the behavior of peace required for soul-mastery. Nonetheless, your leaders and government officials must be made to understand that peace is humanity's *primary* function on planet earth now and that caring must be for all life, not just human.

So, the severity of what will occur in these months and years just ahead will depend on your commitment and actions and on the commitment and actions of all other human individuals. Influence all those you can for peace, but stay with your friends who have also chosen peace and let the others go their own way. It will all work out as it must. Be relaxed and do the best you can at all times. It may be, when you are legally an adult (if you aren't already), that parts of your physical family will go one way and you another. Friends will be replaced by better friends. But always you will be guided. Trust in this. This guidance is your greatest gift while in a human body. For who would deliberately choose to be far from home without a connection to God? This would be a frightening situation for even the bravest of human personalities.

This is not said to frighten you but to indicate the necessity for your commitment to a daily meditation time, or quiet time of contemplation, **without fail** so that you can receive the necessary guidance to be where you should be at all times. Also know that a group meditation is critical, at least weekly.

Then let your meditation or spiritual group form itself into a warm and caring family so you can relax in the sure knowledge that you go on not only with strong earthly companions but also with support from the invisible realms.

Know then that every soul on earth has now been called forth to choose God, with peace as its main function and purpose in life. There will be only three opportunities given each soul to serve God's purposes. Choose wisely now and know joy. For if the changes spoken of must come, they will come primarily to cleanse the earth and this will awaken those who sleep! It may have to shock them into their responsibilities and their soul purpose. Then be awakened now yourself so that you can have certainty, safety, and non-fear in the times *before* the changes come, if they must.

Please know also that even if the unawakened ones should physically die, they will have another opportunity to choose God and to practice peace. These are necessary things to learn and demonstrate, and all earth souls must learn to practice peace, to show caring for all life, and to retain reverence for God.

Be alert to those "on the fence" who might yet see the light; but, after you offer the truth to them, you are not responsible for their choice, only your own. It is easy to become self-righteous but that is not in your best interests. Come from spiritual knowing and discernment, not judgment, and all will be well.

Let it be known that those who acknowledge the light and follow the intention of peace are not to be frightened, because you will be cared for by those of us in the spiritual and angelic realms as you travel the daily events of earth life. You will be given appropriate information if you listen to the messages that will be brought to you regarding the life choices which must be made. Unless there is some major reason why you have agreed to die and leave the planet sooner, it is our intention that you be kept alive to do God's work.

*All souls are required to decide whether they will have peace on earth or not. And each soul is required to make that decision during the Time of Awakening.* If enough people, especially you of the younger ages, decide to have peace and do all you can to obtain it, much of the cleansing can be alleviated. Because of your soul's intention, there is hope; because of your will to serve, there is hope; because of your loving but directed power, there is hope. Then let your courage help reverse the negative thinking of the planet, for even with intense fortitude there can be considerable upset upon the planet during these cleansing upheavals.

You are in a New Age now and there is a Golden Age coming. Then peace will prevail and all beings of goodwill can enjoy each other's company as they build a government which will have a new style of decisionmaking based on true caring and concern. This will be a glorious, very unusual time for those souls who came in the spirit body, then became densely physical, and are now ready to return through spiritual clarity to their former conscious state. In your soul adventure of assisting in the building of this new time you will be guided and protected, rest assured, and your inner knowing will lead the way into the time called The Thousand Years of Peace, or Time of Radiance, which will follow the cleansing time upon the planet.

Not all of the people on the planet will say "Yes" to God's offer. Many will remain asleep, remain negative, for this planet has been undergoing further and further degradation, slipping deeper and deeper into the darkness, with humanity forgetting the Creator-of-All. And so, many souls may find that their commitment to the everyday material world does not include acknowledging God. Thus you may lose certain companions along the way who cannot observe the need for peace and who do not choose to help you turn the world around, so to speak.

About this you can do nothing. Even the Christ consciousness—the Light of God—is powerless to make a person do what is in his/her best interest. Nevertheless, the light forces stand ready to help those who do ask for it. They are not allowed to interfere with or control your free will unless you request it, however. Some people have become so technologically insane that they have invented things worse than the nuclear bomb and seem unconcerned that hydrogen, with which they tamper, could affect the entire Universe with a powerful reaction in space. If your military forces continue to set off hydrogen, nuclear, or atomic explosions within the earth's body, all of you will suffer. **Hydrogen is a building block of the Universe. And such activities endanger life in space as well as life on your planet. Earth people may not harm God's other creations.** Remember that space is filled with energy, webbed together throughout the vastness of the galaxy and beyond, and that any adverse condition on earth can affect other lifeforms.

You are asked to do all you can to stop this insane course being pursued by many in positions of military and governmental power around the planet.

Even in your own family, in your school, and among your friends you must stand forward in clarity for God's purposes to avoid serious planetary repercussions. *Life may hang in the balance for billions.* You need to understand the criticalness of this, because it may not be easy to disagree with those who seem unaware. If they do not share your certainty and you cannot capture their interest to also serve the great Creator, then accept them but always follow your own inner truth.

The people who do have a commitment to God will join together in a very tightly knit bond and those who do not choose peace will tend to draw away from the brightness of your light and the path you follow. They may just drift away, leaving you with your new spiritual friends—rather like oil from water.

26

Know that it was never our intention for the human family to be separated into factions or unloving relationships. But this separation in consciousness will become more pronounced in the days ahead. And during the coming years some may have what is called the physical death of their body as a result of their personality's choice to disregard the soul's call for peace. However, you must believe that this does not obliterate the soul and they will have continuing experiences of consciousness at other levels. So you need not fear for them or yourself. Just be alert and focus on your purpose for peace. Fear freezes you and is a negative response to opportunity. You will be kept advised in your meditation times and in dreams about what is appropriate behavior for you in any given situation.

It is normal for a soul to leave its body at what you call death and make its transition back to God's higher dimensions. Should this comment make you nervous or vulnerable about dying, know that the God you revere is a God who cares and you will be supported in this life, and beyond, to the extent you ask for it.

Your youthfulness and ability to adapt to change are wonderful characteristics that make you extremely useful and helpful to God. For many times, some of the older members of a society get very stuck in their ways of behaving and thinking and find it nearly impossible to change. This is not a blanket statement, but we discern there are such tendencies in many. Fortunate, and appreciated, are the bright-eyed older persons on earth who love God fervently and follow their guidance about life's purpose and activities steadfastly and joyfully.

Take time to feel the meaning of what has been said, and remember that your daily thinking creates the future. Be sure you create what you really want!

To assist you in this Time of Awakening, it is necessary to pay attention to your dreams and quiet meditation times. Be ready to welcome your new friends who will share a common purpose, for this is that time about which all religions have spoken. It is the time when each soul is called forth to make a decision about its willingness to love God and serve the planet as a Caretaker of peace, a preserver of all life.

You must decide for yourself if God does exist and if you wish to relate to this highest of all energies. This is the ideal time to decide for God and be a consistent, steady and reliable server. Vacillation only hinders the process. In this "sorting out" time, please be aware that your consistent behavior is vital. Choose well. Choose the only lifeline that anyone on this planet can have during this time of immense change. Know that, if you choose God, you will be supported in two ways. First, by the spiritual realms or invisible world beyond your sight, and then by those earth-beings in a physical body like your own who are also on the path of God's program. Your earthly meditation groups are *very important*, because you combine your energies from the three-dimensional world with heavenly densities and dimensions to bolster, guide, protect, and care about your growth and service.

Begin your weekly group meditation now and do not let another day go by without joining or starting a group yourself. If you commence with only two people it will surely grow, especially if you risk asking others to come together and if you agree to have peace on earth. It is not difficult to reach out once you know the power that this brings into your sphere of existence. You have been told we would never leave you comfortless, you who have been sleeping. Awaken, then. Move into the greater light. Rejoice with those who will join you in this great endeavor to have preservation of all life upon your planet.

There are many people on earth who are close to this greater love understanding and if *you* model it that remembrance will be called forth in them. So often we see how afraid earthlings are to speak of this thing called peace, yet it is the **most critical issue** of your day. Be honest with others as you share your concern and see if it doesn't frequently elicit a supportive response in them. When it does not, release any concern or upset and fear that you won't be liked and then go your own way. This is the greatest gift you can bring onto the planet. Your certainty and your willingness to be guided by a power superior to your own personality and its many negative barriers are your lifelines now.

This time on earth can be a marvelously joyful time, for it brings to conclusion a long and wearisome venture into the density of material world living. So, know that your soul choice will be heard! Through your meditation, prayer, and contemplation times the security of knowing will be given you—even as dreams may also come to show the way. Be certain that you take time to listen within. By this willingness, this commitment, you can be secure and you will be guided as needed.

Remember the story, or fairy tale, in which Sleeping Beauty lay asleep for eons of time awaiting the kiss of her beloved Prince Charming? You are a symbol of that tale, for the sleeping personality must regain consciousness and it is God's energy kiss that will bring you back to full awareness and purpose. Accept your kiss of awakening then and let its beauty bring you home once again.

By your awakening you can share that sweet kiss with the planet herself and all the life upon it; your glow will brighten the life of all you meet. As the planet is awakened into the higher vibrations of her own destiny, those of you who understand the process can accompany this grand lady on her journey into the higher reality and planes of God-consciousness she has earned—and to which you will have contributed.

There is a plan. The plan says you need do nothing but listen within and ask what you should do. Then follow your guidance. In this way, the guiding hand of wisdom will direct your life into the self-mastery you seek, into the Oneness of all minds with God. You will change from a dense to a higher vibration as your existence is upgraded on the planet by a means you can scarcely grasp. For planet earth is rising, spinning faster! and you accelerate with her. Time, as you know it, moves faster! Simply know this is true. You are a body within a greater unit and she goes forward. This is higher vibration time—a great, wonderful adventure in which you may seek and find God. Your search is over, ones of light. This is the Time of Awakening.

For some souls who are not willing to undertake this Time of Awakening as a growth period for self-mastery and for service to the planet and the Creator there can occur that which is called death. But it will be death of the old ways they have believed and lived. Fresh ideas and willingness to have peace must be instituted, and so that which is in conflict with peace must change, adapt, or fade away from the scene.

For those who try to hang onto material possessions and the ways things have always been, severe emotional pain is probable. If they cannot adapt to new ideas and God's purpose they may also die physically and be seen no more on this planet. For like the dinosaurs of old which could not adapt, events will transpire to remove the rigid and unbending from the challenge they refuse to accept with even a little willingness.

Death is change or transformation, then, and not to be feared by you if you are willing to grow and learn. Are you *willing* to learn more about this life and death cycle on planet earth as it affects you? We hope so. If you are willing, be still and let that inner light always guide you. For within that greater you-of-silence lies God's creation.

# CHAPTER III
# WHAT IS LIFE?
# WHAT IS DEATH?

Most people have never asked themselves what it means to have life, or to be alive. In fact, they are only aware of life when illness, disease or the possibility of death arises. They only reflect on it when they realize they may no longer have it. Consequently they do not see life and death as a continuum, or circle, in which God has arranged a cycle of experiences bridging two worlds. The world of what is called the physical and that which is called the spiritual cannot be separated. They go together.

In your western technological societies especially, death is so greatly denied and feared that life is seldom really understood and infrequently utilized to fulfill the purpose for which it was created. This is probably due in part because people who work in offices all day, or work only with mechanical things, are far removed from the cycles of life that nature presents to those who farm or live in rural areas. In those areas it is much easier to be a part of life and death because these are witnessed in the plants and animals and in the rhythms of growth on a planet which is alive and has its cycles, a planet of which humanity is but one segment. Living close to Mother Earth one can feel connected to her as a link in a greater design.

How do you feel about Mother Earth? About life and death?

There was a pre-humanity time when being alive meant existence only in a spiritual, not a physical, body. When those spiritual beings abandoned their role as Caretakers of the earth and became physically enmeshed with the very creations they had come to observe, assist, and nurture, they lost their God consciousness. Only then did what is now called humanity become susceptible to the process of physical death. **So death is the creation of humanity, not of God.** That is the simple truth.

Now, let us establish a simple definition of life.

Life here on your planet is based upon and relies on energy or electromagnetic power to exist. Nothing can operate without it. If you see something dead it is without any vitality or energy at the physical level. Of course there are greater energies operating your solar system and galaxy and Universe, but for the planet earth we will keep it very simple.

This power, or energy, is furnished by God and is brought down to your low level by many beings of light. This energy is necessary for life to form, continue, and maintain itself. The original body model on earth was a self-maintaining model; within it were all the ways possible to self-clean and self-heal. It was not made to fall apart, to be stressed, or to be abused by toxins brought upon it by its soul occupant. It was very nearly a perfect ongoing machine capable of self-repair.

Through eons of misuse and personal lack of responsibility for its care and keeping, the longevity of body life on your planet has fallen from thousands of years in its duration to less than a one hundred year span for most people. Strange but true, that which you were has become increasingly weak, susceptible to disease, and self-poisoned by the personalities inhabiting these wonders of engineering.

So, what is the situation of life in a body on planet earth these days? It is generally not a long life, nor a healthy one; it is a life frequently filled with disease and pain and deterioration. This brief existence lasts a short blink, even in your time frame and by your measure! Therefore, your time is very precious to you and we recommend you use it wisely.

The battery that keeps your body functioning is not of this material world. It is God-stuff and, unless you meditate and live a life free from self-poisoning, you will not be able to re-fuel it properly and maintain a long, healthy life. There are some small groups on your planet who live long lives of 130-140 years and your scientists are always analyzing them to find out why they live so long. It is not surprising that these are people who work hard, eat simple foods, drink pure water, and avoid the types of self-poisoning perpetuated by western technological life styles.

That is not to say there is no good brought by science. But it does say that science can never substitute for God's energy and God's plan for life. Medicine's role on this planet used to consist of balancing the energies and prevention of disease and deterioration. Now, society and your doctors wait until something happens to an individual and then attempt to deal with a crisis, often self-induced by irresponsible behavior. Some doctors are becoming aware that this is not true medicine and have found a way to bring prevention back into its natural focus. A few western doctors even charge for keeping you well, rather than collecting fees for crisis intervention. There is much to learn from your oriental nations on this topic of energy with which they tend to be more familiar.

Now this energy that God uses to fuel all of life can be seen only by a few clairvoyants on your planet. These people can actually witness the sparkles of light and color around a person's body, or around plants, animals, etc. There was a time, millions of years ago, when everyone could see these light bodies, or auras, around a person.

These energies flow along routes, or roads, called meridians, around the body itself, and are attached to the physical body with a spiritual lifeline or energy hose, connected when an infant is born. It is regrettable that most people cannot see these wonderful energy gifts from God, because it means you are asked to accept many things on faith that formerly were personally experienced by you. You are in a lost world and your planet resides in deep amnesia, a slumber of millions of years of darkness and negativity. For if you could use your sixth sense, as you call it, and could see what is really happening, the task heaven faces in bringing your soul back to full remembrance would be simplified.

There are many books written about this life energy with descriptions of its various colors which you may wish to study, but it is the silvery-white Ray that brings the seven colors of the light spectrum to your third-dimensional level. Little is known of this ray's power and nature; however, just recently the Silver Ray has spoken to humanity and many on earth will now come to know its healing importance.

God's energy—that wonderful substance—is almost iridescent at times as it flows around the body, in and out of your very pores, standing out a foot or more, depending upon your condition of health. As you meditate and visualize the energy forming a large force field around you, this is done according to the pattern you set. And you can draw in God's energy in great amounts, swelling your own energy field out to many feet in all directions. It is as if you were set on low wattage that can be turned up like a three-way light bulb. Which is why meditation is so vital to your everyday life. In the time of your meditation you not only listen to inner guidance, but you can also enlarge and strengthen your energy field which is especially critical during times of stress and strain. For the wider, or more balanced, your energy field is maintained around your body, the better you feel and the easier life is. Many times we have told you that we want you to be happy! Believe it. And by keeping your energy level high, you stay encased in a shining light expression of what you truly are.

Remember, however, that it is you who must bring God's energy to you and keep it there. Angry emotions, depressions, and guilt pull the energy tight around the body, to a very low level, and leave you vulnerable to others' negativity. Like a tank without fuel you will get so empty that the body cells become susceptible to deterioration and illness. Although the body has some energy based on the biochemical nature of its earthly creation, the source of your soul and spiritual nature is God's energy, a different thing altogether. And it is because most people can't see energy that you get into such problems on your planet. Many wonderful spiritual light beings are trying to assist you and you can't even perceive them. Neither can you witness the energy fields of the physical humans like yourself. Have you, in fact, ever seen that God energy and light around *your* physical body?

In the future you will all have knowing of one another by the color, brilliance, and beauty of your auras. For an aura's light shows the true nature of a person and is far more accurate in identifying purposes and values and intentions than looking at the physical body. In the New Age people will be in the open about who and what they are. Secretive deceptions will be harder to manage and so-called confidence men and liars will be easily spotted by those who can see energy. Yet, until you actually have the ability to observe the energy with your physical eyes, you can still feel, sense, or know something, can't you?

These hunches, or bits of intuitive information, come from your inner guidance which reports what is seen, felt, or experienced by being in the other person's aura. Some people are wonderful to have around, even if they do not speak, and others are not at all pleasant energies. When these energy fields intermingle information can be known both from a personal encounter or in group interactions. The energy fields of others are their calling cards if you are at all sensitive to them. For haven't you said, "John certainly has a lot of energy!" or "I don't have any energy today" or "I don't like Mary's energy; it's depressing to be around her"?

Yes, you can know and sense things even if you can't see them. And it is this part of your knowing that we support and encourage in this Time of Awakening.

The importance of meditation or prayer or contemplation times each day is not just to hear inner guidance, but to increase your body's energy supply and maintain the body in a higher ring of light vibration. The higher the energy, the more brightly you shine, and the more likely your body will hum along like a wonderfully tuned airplane or automobile engine. Energy is the key to a happy and enjoyable life. It is health. Those who lack energy are often troubled by a variety of physical complaints, disease, and finally death. For if the body parts are abused from within, by your own negative thinking's influence on the cells, the energy supply can't keep up with the deterioration and the soul finally decides to abandon the particular body it has lived in.

This abandoning of its energy source is death to the body. Yet keep in mind that the "you of the soul" and the "you of God" have lost nothing, for the energy returns to its higher estate, or heavenly home, for other experiences. This is the cycle planned long ago when your spirit bodies came as Caretakers of the earth and left the remembrance of God for a life in the physical denseness of death's vibration.

Be certain you know that the real you is indestructible and that death, as it is called on earth, is simply a release of life energy from a temporary excursion back to its higher homeland. Death is a transition.

The definition of death is easier to comprehend once this cycle of coming and going is clarified. If you have ever travelled from one house to another, or from one city to another, you can understand death. You start from one place, go to another, and return, or continue elsewhere thereafter. Like a trip, life is but a chapter in a book called "time on earth." It is not the whole book. It is related to authorship, however, and to that essence which wrote the book—namely your higher self, or soul. It is as if you wrote a play or TV or movie script, forgot you did it, and then went to the theater to star in it anyhow.

Because your visits to earth are so short these days we urge you to take care of the body you have, whatever its size, shape, or color. It is your ticket to life's experience, your passport to a foreign land from that which is home or heaven. Make the trip worthwhile. Keep your body as safe and healthy as you can while going about the activities of love on this planet. But know that you are more than your body and use it as you would a fine, expensive airplane. Keep it properly fueled, maintained and, if necessary, repaired. As the pilot of your experience, these are responsibilities to be accepted with seriousness and commitment. One does not worship a body but one uses it wisely until its usefulness is over and the soul returns home to seek its next horizon.

You have experienced physical life—its breath, activity, and earth events—but most people do not believe they have experienced death. In fact, most people think of death as something totally foreign, which is amusing, since you presently spend approximately one-fourth to one-third of your earth life asleep or drowsing. And sleep is a leaving of the everyday consciousness and a return to the level of the soul for other services, learnings, and life experiences at a higher, more purified level. So, if you have ever slept, you already know what a "little death" is, though you may not have thought about it that way.

Unfortunately, scientists generally do not explain sleep as a state of consciousness in which higher soul activities are practiced. And so, the mass of humanity believes that it knows nothing about death. Strange that such things are the case here on your earth, but it is our intention that *you*, at least, understand the truth so you are not afraid. Death is a state of reality in which you leave the physical plane, but are alive and functioning elsewhere. So you already know how to leave the body, even if you do not remember it. For don't you return every time you nap or "pass out" or sleep?

If you did not return from a natural sleep, you would be permanently based (or find yourself living) in the world of your full estate, in the mansion of your soul, in the home of truth and certainty. Why, then, does anyone fear death? Death is merely a transferring of your beingness, aliveness, and vitality into a more useful, enjoyable, and fruitful existence. The only difference between sleep and death, essentially, is that in sleep your magnetic thread of energy, along which life energy flows to maintain the physical body machine, is retained, while at death the thread or pathway of energy to the body is permanently released. When this happens you move from one dimension or density vibration to another, always moving higher and higher into the true reality of life.

In its simplest explanation death is a kind of soul graduation out of the physical condition back into one of a spiritual nature. This change can take the soul to a glowing, heavenly place if the individual's vibration and love nature are high.  Or, for those who do not choose God, it could be a continuation of the miseries caused by their earthly beliefs and the negative behaviors—in short, a painful place.  Know that your consciousness of caring for all lifeforms, your desire for peace, and love of God are the keys by which entry is gained into the cosmic territories of the Christ or the Light.

What happens to a body and to its higher self, or soul, at the time of death?  Actually, there is a great deal of misinformation about the experience called death.  So we will begin at a very elementary level and explain the processes for you to grasp.

On the planet earth death comes as sorrow to most beings because they expect to lose something.  Yet the true understanding of death is one of gain.  The greatest challenge, and most difficult acceptance of any earthly attitude you have, surrounds that called death.  Yet this will change as we complete the Time of Awakening, when many may die into a higher estate and a more love-filled reality.  You realize that many cultures have established rituals and funerals connected with that process called death, in which the essential purpose is to honor the departed soul, to give support to the bereaved, and to pray for the safe arrival of the departed into higher dimensions.  Have you ever attended such an event?  How did it make you feel?

Presently on earth there are those who doubt that life continues at all once the body is dead and who expect to be totally annihilated.  Then there are those who believe death is something unknown that they couldn't possibly understand and, therefore, they imagine it to be immensely fearful.  It is regrettable that some humans favor these presumptions for they are not true, and we of the higher realms ask you not to hold either belief.

These primitive attitudes about life and death hold your planet in the darkest of understanding about its most important activities or happenings. Life does continue, be assured of that. And it is God's intention to make you aware of the truth about death and to place it into a framework that allows you comfort and flexibility in your present attitudes. For there may come future occurrences upon the planet in which death is a visitor to be understood, not feared and denied.

We offer clarity that the life you were given early in the creation of souls, or spiritual energies, will continue even without a body. We guide your thinking into the certainty that death is not arbitrary and every soul has its reasons for the type of death it chooses and the time and place of its conclusion. We wish to confirm your identity far beyond this body and this place of present habitation.

Please reread this section about death and what it truly is until you begin to release all falsehoods, fears, and guilts you have been carrying regarding this process of life and death. For it is by your relinquishment of the false information and the acceptance of these more general guidelines that you will come to a knowing place of peace where you are always safe, no matter what is happening to you or around you in other people's experiences.

There is no death, regardless of what you may have believed. Death is a doorway. And if your time to die should present itself, you can relax into it by saying, "I surrender to your will in my life, Creator. Take me home to my highest level." When you know death to be a wonderful doorway, back to greater light and an opportunity of gaining new life experiences of creativity and joy and learning, you will be free to relax and truly live.

In a small corner of your heart you still remember this truth, so let us draw that remembrance forth into the certainty of the

40

conscious mind. When you can trust death to be a positive experience then you really live—you can go forth into any event with security. Today, we hope you will begin to surrender your false beliefs about life and death and receive the true peace and joyfulness that you deserve.

When physical death finally occurs the soul leaves the body. The life current loses its active, energizing quality, the aura ceases, and the body becomes a dead or inactive unit or machine. Let us be sure you understand this.

The body chemicals normally hang in suspension for six to eight hours until the final soul decision to depart is made. Many soul departures are confirmed in these hours so there is no need for a longer suspension period in the body. There have been occasions when 14 hours were allowed a soul to decide about departing from the planet, and a rare instance of 18 hours. This is not recommended, however, due to body or tissue changes.

Near the time of death there is a review of the life. If life is to be continued on earth the soul acts differently after the deliberation, because it has received specific information and tasks to accomplish and comes back with certainty and clarity of purpose. If life is not to be continued, physical death occurs.

The process of physical death is complete when the soul leaves, the energy ceases to flow, and the physical body becomes very cold. Anyone looking at the body, or being in its presence, is aware of the lifelessness in the body machine. Like a car permanently without a battery, it is no longer useful for transportation. What is done with the physical body at that time is of no importance to the departing soul and rests with the customs or wishes of the family and friends who had earth attachments to the deceased.

*Any prayers or petitions should be for the soul's safe passage and for letting go of connections to the earthly level. This* letting go is vital because the soul goes through a review period with an evaluation group which involves the discussion and examination of the years spent in earthly existence. If urgently necessary, an immediate return will be instituted into either a new birth or taking over a currently available body, but this is a rarity. Normally there is a resting period.

Most often this evaluation and review is not started until three days have passed from the time of death. The soul is allowed this time for saying goodbye or completing unfinished jobs or duties on the earth plane.

Those departed souls who do not "let go" after the three days, or sooner if desired, cause difficulties for themselves and those connected to them on the planet. There must be an acceptance of the changes involved. We understand there is emotional pain connected to your earthly existence, especially at the death of a loved one, but we try to send other persons and activities to fill the empty space left by this situation. *We want you to be happy.*

Do not hang onto grief like a rock around your neck. Honor the dead, but honor yourself as well. Grieve and then release yourself from it. Your belief that you must continue to grieve for an entire year or longer is not valid. One could begin to feel good about life again after about three months if the proper attitude were maintained about what life and death truly are. Your habits and beliefs that you cannot, or do not wish to, survive without the other person lock you into the pain. Pain comes from attachment. Attachments occur because you have asked another to bring you joy, serve your needs, and fill your life with value. There is nothing wrong with sharing and loving. But if you totally depend upon others for your needs and happiness, pain will ensue should they die. Relationships are natural, necessary, and a vital part of the earth plane existence, but you waste inordinate amounts of time on past attachments once events which terminate a relationship have transpired. By doing so you preclude new experiences in the present and deny the future's promises. Your emotions become unbalanced and you may fall victim to depression and never ending cyclical sadness. This is foolish and extremely painful.

Surprising as it may seem to you, earth was created as a true paradise. It was never meant to be painful and full of suffering for its inhabitants. If your life has been that way you may wish to examine the thought patterns you hold that bring this experience to you. Yes, there are lessons to be learned but they can be acquired quickly and do not demand the pound of flesh your own guilt creates. Pain is actually a reversed use of the emotional nature given you to appreciate God, your planet, and all lifeforms. We watch in dismay the beings of earth who grovel in years of emotional pain instead of opening up to emotional joy and harmony. And in answer to the anguished calls that come to us for help and respite, we share these truths of living to assist humanity. They are seldom used, unfortunately. Seldom is the advice taken. And the continuing emotional disharmony is never resolved for many. This brings about the need for repetitive earth lives.

In the Time of Awakening, however, every soul on the planet will have the opportunity to hear the inner voice speak of God's purpose and of each soul's responsibility—both individually and in groups—to create peace, which is the basis of joy and the reverse of pain.

Your pain is caused because you are not peaceful. Examine this negative cause and change it! This is your present task. Then let peace on earth and reverence for all lifeforms on the planet send a loving call to the Creator. It is time to have gentle thoughts and wonderful experiences. How far your lives have strayed from the original pattern! Do not delay the acceptance that something more beautiful exists. Commit your life to the peace and caring expected of you as an earth dweller.

Earth is a school for learning the lesson of loving God, of nurturing the planet and its life, and of respecting others who live with you on this free will spaceship. Love does not mean possessiveness and attachment. Love is freely given without what you call "strings" and expectations.

Life on earth starts with a lowering of soul energy into the third-dimensional realm in order to learn those great lessons of love and service. These lessons all have to do with that rule given many times, in many ways—"Love one another! Do unto others as you would have them do unto you." In all ways, these lessons are your basic moral guidelines. When life is lived in a way that expresses unconditional love, a higher grade or level of consciousness is attained, and the soul grows, flowers, and builds an energy pathway to even higher and higher levels where that love is refined and expressed more glowingly.

The body is very dense in energy vibrations, of course, and limits your direct experience of light and pure love. Since your body is the receptacle which bears the result of your mind thinking and heart feeling, it is your "mind over matter" suit. The body constantly demonstrates what you are thinking, however, and ranks or rates your understanding and expression of love. To think of your body in any other way is a limitation.

The body tells you how you're doing. That is why the use of drugs, alcohol, and other forms of distortion are dangerous. They cloud the purity of your soul and mind and lead to the pain and suffering of cause and effect unrecognized. For what you do must return to teach you something about love, even if it is only respect and love for the physical body you were given to take care of in this life. Those who misuse their bodies must be willing to experience the pain and suffering that go with an unloving act.

To restate what has been said, physical life is a time and place where you live not remembering where you spend the other third or fourth of your time. It is for most humans an amnesialand. So use your dreams or ask in meditation to know what you do elsewhere, in that vacationland, your true home, away from earth life. Ask to dream and remember and understand. In meditation, draw near to the source of that other, true identity and bring more of it with you into the physical world.

This veil, or covering, between what seems to be real and what is the actual reality is much like a play, a TV show, or a movie. While here, you are on stage in a learning mode. When it is time to leave the theater and go home, you merely leave, knowing that a timed event is over. Let death be the same! Acknowledge that your consciousness is best used at the higher dimensions again when the soul of greater knowing releases the bond or connection to earth. Let your deceased physical vehicle lie in peaceful repose. Let the truth of your highest purpose and knowledge take full control once again. You are not just your body. Use it well and with appreciation, but do not worship it unless you want to experience the pain such an attitude will bring.

When your trip to earth has been a full and valuable learning experience and the pattern of love is even more fully realized and expanded, the visitation to a lower life adventure will be over. Don't do anything to hasten the natural unfoldment of that process called death! Do not interfere by changing your soul's blueprint of the spiritual drama in which you agreed to star. Do not abuse your body, mind, or emotions. Let this be your guideline and the life you lead will bring great joy and fulfillment. Why ignore or misuse your opportunity? Why lose the respect and appreciation that a job well done affords?

For the average "good" citizen, death is only a continuance of the living process where the interests or tendencies of life are carried forward. And you will not sense much difference if your life has been a balanced one, if you have given love and served the world in caring and concern. Your credentials from earth life present themselves long before the moment of death, don't they? For you have been on "the other side" during sleep in all the years of your earth life.

Death is an automatic and nearly immediate entrance into a greater sphere of learning, growth, and service to which you are well-accustomed already. You then simply live at that higher level of purpose, joy and understanding. Nonetheless, while you are here, earth is a homeland that requires your care and service. Treat all life with respect. Live as peacefully as you can and help others do the same. This is the reason for your earth visit—to love the planet, all of life, including animals, plants, trees, flowers, birds, sea creatures, gems, minerals, and even rocks. For all of that was planned for your healing and enjoyment and was placed in your hands to care for long, long ago.

Complete your mission wisely so that you maintain self-respect and a sense of worthiness. Be willing to let the great soul-of-you lead the way by establishing a time of daily listening which will aid you in constantly remembering your journey's purpose, your heart's delight. As you join daily with the greater YOU of God's expression, you will stop thinking of death as a catastrophic event and can assist others to cope with their fear or even terror of death.

Death is not an entrance into uncertainty, nor a sudden loss of experience and joy. But because of humanity's instinct for survival, most people think it to be so. Nearly all of you on earth live in a constant state of fear that you will be snuffed out, somehow, and extinguished from the familiarity of what you value. Accept that there is a steadfast and certain law in charge of the Universe and know that you are part of its process. Trust that and you will know peace. When you can truly say, upon your natural death, "God, take me to my highest state of being for peace and joy," you can rest easily about your return from material body form into the glowing world of magnificence and radiance. Trust that light and energy which keep your solar system and your galaxy growing and expanding.

There is nothing of intrinsic value to lose by what you call death. There is truly nothing to fear. Know that and you will have peace. Know that and you will have life abundantly.

Ask your higher self if this is the truth for you.

# CHAPTER IV
# PERSONAL AND PLANETARY SUICIDE

We have explained what natural death is. Now we speak about unnatural death, or what you call suicide. This we do because we are concerned about the rising suicide rate among young people; therefore, we speak now about the act of suicide, or unnatural death, and its negative effects upon the soul.

For you, on earth, adolescence and early adulthood are often experiences of confusion and turmoil, because you are learning to carry out earth responsibilities, establishing your vocation or profession, your marriage or home life, and interacting in a variety of relationships. There are many decisions to be made regarding an unknown future.

It is also a time when, if you are still living with your parents, you are subject to their decisions and style of living. This can be joyful or painfully difficult. If there is frequent quarreling or a divorce, emotional instability, illness, neglect, criminal behavior, or extreme conditions of physical or sexual abuse in the family unit, a young personality can become depressed and feel deserted. There are as many different family situations as there are people. No two are precisely identical. And each one is a special "soap opera" designed by its participants either knowingly or unknowingly, consciously or unconsciously.

Young adults may not be willing to understand or appreciate that they have chosen their specific parents and their life situations, but it is true. The family you are a part of is the relationship you chose before birth to help you fulfill your soul's contract with God. They are the models you wanted to grow up with. From them you can learn much that is needed by your soul to fulfill its purpose. This is probably a very provocative idea, especially for those of you who are living in unpleasant circumstances.

Besides the experiences you are gaining from your present family situation, you are also having your individual experiences of success or failure in school work, of being part of your peer group, of finding out what personal love is all about, and of learning to deal with loneliness.

The greatest loneliness of all is separation from a belief in God. Many young people know they are hungry for something that they never seem to find. The object of their seeking is God, if they but knew it, for in making that connection every situation and event in your earth journey is supported by wise and caring help from the realm where your true identity lies: your *spiritual* home.

While you are here on earth in your practice lessons, learning to deepen your understanding of love, however overwhelming the experiences seem to be, know that *you* chose most of them. *Know also that you must ask for help when you need it, because this is a free will planet.* Therefore, learn to ask for help from God, and also from others in earthly form—to smooth the way and guide you wisely and caringly through your life. Then, even if you consider suicide as a means of escape, you will never actually commit that self-destructive act because you will be certain to receive help; then life will be better. Those who are alienated from God have no spiritual support; they suffer intense pain, because isolation and separation are unnatural states of being. This pain and refusal to reach out for help bring depression and emotional defeat to many people, but especially to the young.

Because there are people on earth who love God and have made their life commitment to helping other humans on the planet, you will want to invite their assistance. These beings are often found in the capacity of teachers, counselors, psychologists, ministers and spiritually oriented people, or maybe they just appear as a loving older person in your family, or a personal friend who loves you.

So even if you become addicted to drugs or alcohol, or have intercourse leading to disease or unwanted pregnancy, or commit criminal acts—all is not lost. You do not need to kill yourself in order to escape from such a situation. Often humans must learn the hard way *rather than by accepting God's guidance.* No matter how awful the past, though, every moment is a new beginning. We would suggest you remember that *there is no condition love cannot cure!* Naturally, it is better not to get yourself involved in a situation which will bring you pain and suffering, but even unpleasant experiences can help you develop and grow. In every situation you have a choice: you can exercise discernment by choosing pleasant and positive experiences, or you can allow yourself to become the "victim" of your own undisciplined, negative behavior. We recommend that you ask for guidance in all your planning and decision making. Seek support from the God forces all the years you live.

To receive either spiritual help from God or earthly help from humans you are required *to ask for help* because this is a free will planet and choosing wisely is your responsibility in all your affairs. Help comes from talking to your own soul, to God and other great ones created by God, and to the invisible teachers, angels, and guides given you at birth. These, plus

your earthly associates, are a team to see you through a successful life experience. **You never need to be alone. You can
always count on help, if you ask for it.**

That is why suicide is so needless. But worse than that, suicide is an act that ignores God's law regarding life. Put simply,
that law is: PRESERVATION OF ALL LIFE UPON THE
PLANET AND PEACE ON EARTH. This principle underlies
the Golden Rule, the Ten Commandments, and the noble truths
taught by all the earth's major religions.

For the awakened person suicide is totally unthinkable, for a
variety of reasons. As just mentioned, it violates the universal
law regarding the preservation of all life, and thereby seriously
deters the soul's growth. Much effort and planning goes into a
life journey, and there is a definite contract made by the soul
with God regarding its growth requirements. Suicide unilater-
ally cancels that contract with God. Finally, it robs the soul of
time to achieve its learning because an entire life is wasted! To
kill yourself is to flunk a course before you have even started.
It is like refusing to take a course required for graduation.

Not only does the soul miss its own growth lessons, it also
abandons an opportunity to serve humanity and planet earth
which is part of every soul's responsibility.

Besides missing their own opportunity for personal advancement and their chance to serve the planet and humanity,
those who kill themselves cause pain and anguish for the personal family and friends who remain. These are left without a
needed member of their learning group—a soul comrade is
missing! So suicide also emotionally hurts the human personalities left behind, not just the one abandoning life. Family,
friends, and other associates are left to ponder the "why" and
perhaps to accuse themselves of being responsible somehow.
Parents, particularly, can suffer agony over a child's suicide.
Think of these things, then, and vow to see life through to the

very end, no matter what is going on. And always use the advice of your spiritual helpers in the heavenly domains and those of earth who would also assist. To do less than this during your earth adventure is to deliberately go naked into a raging blizzard. Earth is a testing ground or a school for love. Be prepared to do your best and commit your life to the God who created you. This will bring you joy and wonder and satisfaction. Every religion on earth speaks of that peace which surpasses all words and understanding. This, we hope you know, is the *peace of God*, which must be sought and accepted.

According to the statistics regarding young adult behavior in western countries, and from what we also observe, the majority of young people lacks peace and operates in confusion without spiritual direction. The suicide rate upon the planet, especially in the so-called technological countries, is high and rising. It is highest among the 15 to 24 year old group with no apparent decline in sight, which is one reason why we are issuing this information. *We are very concerned about this negative trend!*

In the American age group of 15 to 24 year olds alone, about 5,500 actually kill themselves each year and one-half million try it. This is out-and-out suicide by firearms, poison, or other methods equally deliberate. However, you of earth have many other ways of destroying yourselves by the personal habits you allow to run rampant, such as drinking alcohol and taking what are called the illicit drugs. These toxins, such as cocaine, marijuana, and other stimulants, are abusive to your body. They also affect the nervous system and the emotional reactions you bring to life circumstances. These are types of *indirect* suicide.

It appears to us that young Americans, between the ages of 13 and the mid-twenties, are great experimenters. They can hardly resist a dare, a challenge, or a peer group's demand for

53

conformity. Thus, about three-fourths of American youths have tried some of the illicit drugs, including those of the marijuana plant, while approximately half of all U.S. youths have tried cocaine or other debilitating stimulants.

One in every 15 to 20 youths drinks alcohol daily and, of those, possibly 35-40% consume as many as four to six (or more) stupefying drinks! This leaves them unreliable in their judgment, driving ability, and other earthly activities. Accident rates increase while drinking. Also, the majority of youthful suicides are committed under the influence of alcohol, for alcohol is a *depressant*.

This trend toward alcoholism and drug misuse can be a type of *direct* suicide, although for most humans it will happen in stages rather than in one direct act of self-murder. This is why the teenage experimentation with alcohol and drugs is a dangerous pattern. Take a good look at your health and life and determine that a few moments' thrill is too high a cost to pay for addiction to chemical substances.

Since you were given a physical body in which to learn, love, and serve, please use it for the original purpose. Do not inflict numbness and toxicity on your physical organs, as that will take its toll on you, your family, social groups, your nation and planet, and even in the spiritual domains, as well. A soul can scarcely function in a physical body when the body is doped up, over or under-stimulated, and essentially unconscious.

*This matter of suicide, direct or indirect, is of great concern to us in the spiritual realms.*

So, although you may be depressed, or experience serious emotional upsets due to the events that seem to hold you in their sway, *please do not kill yourself.* Suicide destroys an irreplaceable body created by God and is to be avoided at all costs. If you are upset, hurt in body or emotions, ask for help from those on the earth and those in higher dimensions. We will assist you in maintaining your commitment to physical life even when things seem darkest. Nonetheless, *it is the responsibility of each human being to care for this body-gift so preciously created.* That being so, it is up to you *never* to deliberately use substances which could kill or injure your particular temple or body—that form created to give you a vehicle through which you can evolve back to a higher knowingness of God.

As the human body grows from its time of conception through the ages of 26 to 28 years, it is sometimes impossible for a person to stay emotionally balanced. This is caused by the physical changes during growth that also involve chemical adjustments in the body machine, primarily through the endocrine system. In addition, some of the body chemicals may be knocked off-balance due to improper health habits. Overeating or overindulging in sugar or "sweet things" causes obesity, hypoglycemia, and diabetes—a fast-rising medical problem.

Often these internal chemical imbalances contribute to emotional problems for young adults, such as "feeling different" from others and lacking the sweetness of life. To compensate for these feelings they will often gorge on food or indulge indiscriminately on the toxic sugary substances, which only makes their difficulties worse. If drugs or intoxicating beverages are turned to, you can be certain that your body chemistry will go, as you say, haywire. Avoid this to have wellness of body.

You are probably expecting from us a caution to avoid smoking tobacco or other substances because these *are* foreign to the body and not beneficial to it in any way! Your lungs were not made to have cigarette smoke inhaled, especially the high quantity which you call "several packs" a day. Continued smoking invites such ailments as emphysema and other lung diseases. These are really suicidal conditions, often terribly painful in their final stages, and we therefore ask you to avoid them by abstaining.

For those who are not willing to care for God's body-gift, there will be problems and pain, because it was created by the Godhead as a place for the soul to live. If you—the personality—affect your body adversely through lack of care, the body will develop difficulties, just as a fine automobile or an airplane would.

Be responsible for eating a nutritious, light diet without additives and preservatives. Eat fresh food instead of "junk," dead items, or packaged foods, that lack the enzymes required for growth and good health. Avoid non-nutritious food and beverages, then, if you want a healthy body. Also get plenty of rest and exercise. *And above all stay emotionally balanced.* With this caring viewpoint and behavior your body will serve you well. But this is common knowledge on your planet, if not common practice.

It is particularly important that you not harm your body temple in this Time of Awakening, a time when God's intention is for the body to be raised in vibration and for the cells themselves to be changed. This is necessary for humanity's next stage of evolution. Do not ignore the possibility that your body can, and will, undergo changes for your spiritual betterment. This is what God has ordained and what your soul has agreed to experience.

Put another way, let us imagine that you have been lowered in a heavy diving suit, hundreds of feet below the water's surface. You can be retrieved from your rather helpless situation only by those above you in a boat who have the equipment and intention to bring you up. But the helpers know they cannot bring you up too quickly or they will kill you. Your body was not built to withstand the sudden change of such pressure, so they must take time to slowly return you to the boat. In a similar way, spiritual evolution occurs in the physical body as well as for your soul. Since you cannot return to the higher vibrations all at once, you need a physical body to maintain your soul while this process is being accomplished.

Your cooperation is necessary in seeing the body as part of evolution's journey, though you are not to deify the body nor get its value out of proportion. You are merely to use it wisely and follow simple instructions regarding its treatment. After this time of vibrational change lies another stage of higher development. So retain a body during this process, since you have agreed in your soul blueprint to do that, and do not commit suicide through the use of drugs, weapons, or other actions that will prevent you from staying on the planet at this critical time of learning.

In this Time of Awakening there will still be the usual so-called earthly temptations and thrill living which create exposure to serious sexual diseases. But you do not have to hurt yourself by careless, foolish behavior. We are asking you to choose a way of life that supports your spiritual awareness and focuses your energy on the constructive acts of life. This is not to say you shouldn't have fun, or sexual expression with a beloved, but we suggest you find joy in the positive processes of life that extend and support harmony, peace, and goodwill—that provide *emotional balance*.

We have mentioned many circumstances that lead to depression and possibly even suicide. But other equally destructive influences are not always clearly defined. We find and observe that, in so-called modern times, television has a great negative influence on the minds and emotions of all humans, especially young adults. This generally negative influence starts when children are very small. For many of them, it continues through their entire lifespan. People worry about robots taking over their work, but it is humans who are becoming robots. God made humans unique with their human emotions so they could become wise and joyful in the ways of universal love, not bitter, angry, and violent. But many have become emotionally desensitized. They have become callous to violence, to hurting other humans and the animal kingdom, and to destroying the planet itself. Due to this immense lack of concern and respect the theme for earth at this time is: PRESERVATION OF ALL LIFE! PEACE ON EARTH! Remember that the preciousness of life itself has to be appreciated! The preciousness of life in a human body has to be appreciated!

We have noted how many young adults are quick to put the blame for their own difficulties upon others and ignore self-responsibility for the situations they find themselves in. The parents are usually blamed first, then the teachers, perhaps other adults, schoolmates or those out in the work field. It is commonly their boss or their place of employment which is said to be unsuitable, while in fact there is not a willingness to fully participate and keep the contract for which they were hired, whether it was written or verbal. There is little respect expressed.

We advise you that in this Time of Awakening you must be responsible for what you think, say, and do, because preservation of life, improvement in the quality of life, and development of the spiritual nature of each human being, is each soul's present theme. This begins with *reverence*, or great respect, for God's creations.

Many times you have heard the word "reverence." That is an attitude which is almost nonexistent on earth. Many people give it lip service but have no heart-felt sense of it. Yet reverence for God is vital. Through that comes self-caring and then caring for others, for the planet, and for the myriad forms of life upon it.

We have observed that some young adults, though not wanting to cease living at their soul level, give up at the *personality* level. Here they seem unable to find the emotional strength to continue living. They lack discipline. Very few of those who kill themselves do it only to hurt other people. Rather, most suicides are caused by deep inner pain and great insurmountable sadness. However, the consequences of suicide will only bring greater sadness. The person who suddenly dies in a suicidal way leaves the body to exist in **a semi-limbo state—a condition which is neither alive in a body nor alive in the spiritual realms.** Instead, for hundreds of years (earth time) the being must be rehabilitated to understand God's principle of *life.* Truly this is most miserable, because the soul in this half-dimensional reality has knowledge and awareness that the suicide was an unwise action. In this place, where the truth of the soul's purpose is clear and the failure of the personality to persevere looms large, pain is frequent in spite of the many caring ones who teach, soothe, and attend the being that is neither of earth nor heaven.

The soul becomes tormented because it has left earth and can't return—neither can it go on to a higher level due to the negative vibrations it carries.

The soul does not necessarily feel guilt, but rather a sadness for not fulfilling the life journey contract that would have brought growth and service. There is generally deep disappointment with this lack of fulfillment, especially when it is seen that the suicide was unnecessary—when it is realized that, if the person had just made a simple change or taken a slightly different path, the life would have been so beautiful, so joyous, and so complete. For in this half-way place a suicide sees the truth—sees the way it could have been if discipline and determination had been used.

*Never commit suicide as a solution to sadness or emotional problems, unless you are willing to accept the soul penalties.* This is because the soul has contracted or agreed to spend a certain time upon the planet and this agreement is to be honored, except in very rare and unusual circumstances.

*On earth you will make mistakes!* This is part of learning, but mistakes are not grounds for suicide. Many youthful suicides have become critically unbalanced in their attitudes and emotions and have rashly overreacted to some unpleasant life experience. If you are miserable in your work, or in your personal relationships where negative events keep occurring, you can make changes to avoid similar encounters. Learn and grow and change. Then learn some more! But never let apparent problems drive you to suicide!

How often in your papers do you read of a suicide and hear people say, "I don't know why he (or she) did that." Often it makes absolutely no sense to those who are left. Even if someone offers reasons such as "He hadn't been getting good grades in school" or "She and her boyfriend had a big fight," these are not sufficient cause for the taking of one's life.

Let us suppose that two married people decide to get a divorce. One does not wish to have a divorce and panics at the thought of what this will mean. A dose of sleeping pills is taken and the person—even if s/he does not wish to die at the very last moment—has set into action an irreversible chain of events for which s/he is responsible.

As soon as death occurs and the being's soul is out of the body into that limbo state, the individual can see immediately the pointlessness of the self-murder in its full context. Perhaps there was to be a later reconciliation, or possibly the divorce would have turned out to be a good thing for both parties. But there is no going back to continue with the experience s/he could have had. It is finished, and the opportunity for a number of learning lessons is surrendered. Someday these lessons must be assumed again! and completed!

Meanwhile, there have to be adjustments made before the soul's evaluation and release from the self-imposed limbo can happen. Since suicides generally stay in that "band" of reality for an extended period of time before they go through a cleansing and a soul adjustment at another level, there cannot be an immediate return to the earth plane. It is not unusual for a suicide to incarnate an additional five to eight lives just to attain harmony and balance again.

The perception after death of what the being has created for itself usually is not a happy one. **This is not punishment. It is the accruing of effects from one's own actions.** This cause and effect principle is called by many words in many languages; it is most frequently spoken of as "karma." A human being's responsibility to be aware of the importance of life is taught in the religions of most every belief system on earth.

The instruction to every person on planet earth is still, *do not kill!* And if that instruction is ignored, the soul must be cleansed of the negative emotions and lack of discipline that brought the incorrect action. The action of suicide, or self-murder, is not spiritually allowable. We ask that you live by this rule: Life is precious and should not be wasted.

The principle, again, is not to shorten the life you were given through unbalanced emotions, hopelessness, and undisciplined behavior. Under your soul's contract with God it is expected that your full life span will be completed as planned and, if you get disturbed and need help, that you will ask for God's help, and human help as well.

From the higher spiritual realms, looking down, we see that most negative situations experienced by individuals, or by humanity as a whole, can be changed once it is recognized what needs to be corrected. And with help all of these situations can be changed. So ask for help when it is needed. Asking for help is the step or process that makes a new opportunity of thinking and feeling available. Yes, change is required, and the greatest change each human on earth must make is to accept that God has a plan for the planet. This plan is not yours to design, but yours to follow. Every soul that resists or ignores that truth will experience pain until it learns otherwise.

This acceptance of God and God's plan may require efforts the personality does not wish to make. Yet each person on your planet is given freedom to do what s/he chooses. But that gift of free will, if used improperly, will teach a harsh reality. Do not allow an act of suicide to cancel your "soul contract" and miss a valuable opportunity to grow.

A "soul contract"? Let us explain.

Before the soul comes to this planet there is a discussion in which the soul learns what a body is and how it can be used to fulfill or acquire certain attitudes, beliefs, or traits that are needed to balance out the completeness of the soul as a thing of beauty and usefulness to God. Although there are a few dissimilarities in the size, shape, and condition of various bodies, they are all godly creations and operate in a fairly standard fashion. The basic functioning of a body is understood by the soul before it comes to earth.

The soul contract, then, is an agreement to gain the experience needed by the soul for its advancement, using a human body on the planet earth as the vehicle, or mode, of attaining that experience. There is a thorough explanation of what the soul is expected to do, and when the soul is ready, a contract is made. This is not forced upon the soul but is rather like an offer of employment—a chance to advance one's level of attainment, or an opportunity for a better future. Know that all of

Spirit is in evolution and therefore is constantly undergoing change. If you can grasp this idea you will be well on your way to understanding why suicide is not an appropriate ending of a soul's contract.

Yes, you agreed to come to earth for your own advancement and also to serve God and humanity and the planet itself. You came as a Caretaker of the earth in its terrible time of difficulty. While you may not consciously remember this, you did attend such a meeting at the soul level and you did have full knowledge of what this life visit was for and its purpose in God's plan on this extraordinarily beautiful planet called earth. To renege on your pledge to grow and serve, by committing suicide, will later be extremely painful.

There are others like yourself who also agreed to come for both growth and service and they, too, are here upon the planet going through the particular things they agreed to experience. Some of them are members of your spiritual family, and they and you have a mutual task of service for the planet and humanity as well as for your individual selves. When you meet such a person you have a wonderful rush of joy and you may feel as if you have known him/her forever. More than you may realize, you did know the person before. And in your coming together—first in your own relationship, and then as part of a group—you are finding your comrades in soul purpose.

Such intense recognition is instantaneous, often overwhelming, but is not to be confused with a bodily or sexual urge. It can happen between the same sexes, opposite sexes, the young and old, those of different colors, countries, or languages. It knows no boundaries or confines, except those which are brought by personality barriers. On a lesser scale this is the same feeling one can have for God and the invisible beings of Spirit. It is the one we would hope you might have for all of humanity, as well. It is a recognition of life and your purpose on the planet, for there is practically no one here who does not have both growth opportunities and service agreements simultaneously.

During this Time of Awakening, particularly, when all souls have been called forth to their soul's contract or service agreement, there will be great stirrings and changes as the barriers and resistances of the personality come under the soul's focused attention. And in this time period, you will either complete your soul contract or face the consequences of that avoidance. You came to be Caretakers of the planet and all life upon it. This, then, is your task and your joy. Nothing else will bring so much spiritual, mental, or emotional fulfillment to a soul and its human personality than accomplishment of the soul's greater commitment.

The major problems which can occur in fulfilling a soul's contract are many and varied; in fact, it is almost impossible for a soul's assignment to work out 100% perfectly as it unfolds. This is so because this is a free will planet and every being on it makes free will choices. Attitudes of an entire group or race or culture have mighty power over the lives of the individuals in it. That is why a democratic country is the best place in which to live while completing the soul's mission, because political liberty provides the greatest opportunity for its subjects to make the free will choice for God. In democracies censorship is avoided and spiritual information is widespread.

Even in the non-democratic countries, however, many will remember their purposes and will come forward to complete them. The soul's influence cannot be contained by physical or political barriers, because it has a greater home and a greater knowing. This greater knowing is the hallmark of an awakened soul.

In the soul contract, then, events may be accelerated for some individuals or held back for others by outer influences. And in the realm of God-knowing, some souls may be swifter or slower than others in remembering their purpose and willingness to pursue it. These variations between people may create confusion in the plans you have in common with other members of your spiritual family.

When a large percentage of humanity forgets its purpose and falls into the deep darkness of spiritual forgetfulness, wars and violence and misery of indescribable horror follow. This is **planetary suicide** in the making. It is during such times that the great teachers and saviors of souls come forth to bring an intensified light and recollection of purpose to stir the individual souls into remembrance and action.

Your planet, the darkest in your particular solar system, is now undergoing such a time. In this Time of Awakening, however, it is not just one great soul who has come to call you forth in awakening—but the two very first creations of God—the Gold and Silver Rays.

Why are these dual God-energies on earth at this time? Because the messages of the great teachers and saviors have not been followed, and war—with further horrendous weaponry in the making—continues and threatens to endanger other life in space. That, dear ones, is why your soul is being called forth, along with every other being upon this planet, to revere God. For either all will come forward to execute their soul missions for peace on earth and the preservation of all life, or there will be a separation between those who will carry out their responsibilities and those who won't. In either case the result will be the same. *Your planet will be peaceful.*

The process of gaining that planetary peace, however, can either be a joyful one for humanity or one of suffering. An important cause of the suffering can be traced to the lack of re-

65

sponsibility among the general citizenry for the attitudes and practices of industry, the governments, and the military. Humanity's general relinquishment of responsibility has resulted in too much negative power being taken by the few who have chosen to ignore God's principle of peace. The mass of humanity sleeps through self-made crises while a few madmen plan major wars, even nuclear or hydrogen extinction. If you would assist us in this Time of Awakening, you must stay alert to these facts.

Your task is to bring yourself back to peaceful intention and to an appreciation of life for humanity and all forms on earth, including the plants and flowers, the animals, minerals, birds, sea creatures, and the very planet you reside upon, too. For unless this measure of peace is established *very soon*, painful events will be experienced on the planet which *humans will have caused themselves*. So do not be led off course. *You are important as a leader and a teacher and a bringer of peace.* Do all you can, knowing that other humans here have the right to avoid their responsibilities and to bring soul pain upon themselves. But know also that they can immediately *awaken* and change the course of earth's apparent destiny. There is great hope that this will occur now with your willing dedication and effort. **Peace is possible!**

You once had an American president who told you not to ask what your country could do for you, but what you could do for your country. The same is now suggested at a higher level. "Ask not what the Universe can do for you, but determine what you will do for the Universe, for your galaxy, for your solar system, and for that great energy known as God." We of the higher realms will absolutely aid you when you ask what you can do, but please do not ask and then make a commitment which you break. Your soul purpose is not served by inconsistency and wavering.

If you are meditating daily by yourself and weekly in a group, you can stay in tune with your soul and its greater contacts in the Universe. You, at least, will be guided no matter what other souls decide regarding their agreements with God. Certainly you will reach out and do your best to awaken other personalities to their souls' missions. But be sure your own spiritual house is in order first and all else will follow. In that way you will complete your soul contract regardless of what others do.

Everyone on this planet has the same number of days in a year and the same number of hours in a day. Yet these hours are spent so unconsciously and negatively by most that the planet has fallen into very low vibrations. Earthlings must awaken! This unconsciousness must change, for we will not lose this garden planet. Hear and remember. The forces of God will not allow humanity to destroy earth or make it a base of negative operation to harm the rest of your solar system, the Milky Way galaxy, or life beyond that. This was done once before and the debris of that hydrogen explosion scattered the planet Maldek into what you call an asteroid belt. Debris and shock waves ripped through space and adversely affected life far beyond the destroyed planet. PLANETARY SUICIDE WILL NEVER BE ALLOWED AGAIN. *Even the potential of planetary suicide must be removed.*

So your soul purpose and contract are not just for serving your own life on this wee planet in the 12th Universe. They must be committed to the rehabilitation of human consciousness that has gone astray. Your life and your planet are small aspects of a greater body, beyond that which you see and to which you gradually return through your soul's awakening.

Shake off the vapor that surrounds your spiritual, mental, and emotional identity and move forward into life which is based on light, not darkness. Help others do the same, if they will, because this cloud of ignorance is contaminating you, your planet, and other life in space, also. *There must be planetary and personal aliveness, not suicide.* Surrender fear, guilt, and unconsciousness, and rise to the achievement of glory. You are a new breed for this New Age. You are peace bringers.

*Personal* suicide is a form of killing or murder which wastes an entire lifetime opportunity, due to a person's foolishness. *Planetary* suicide is the extinction of billions, or more, lifeforms for the same reason. Let us agree you will experience neither!

As the Silver Ray has said:

*We acknowledge the sadness that is behind personal suicide. We acknowledge the sense of hopelessness a person may have. We acknowledge s/he temporarily cannot see any way out of life's problems. We acknowledge all the things humans are feeling. We would never deny or remove those human feelings and emotional factors. However, the advice, recommendation, or suggestion that we would bring is—ASK FOR HELP! Bring your emotions into balance.*

*Say, "I need God's help," in whatever words you use for that. And then specifically outline the kind of help you are asking for. A human being must sometimes allow as long as a three month period of earth time for a complicated situation to be resolved, because if you are in a situation that took years to create, it may not be possible for an immediate and perfect conclusion to be rendered in your thinking overnight. Although The Christ and I offer that instantaneous gift of healing, most humans resist any type of instant change. Only a few believe that if they change their mind today all traces are immediately forgiven and forgotten. Instantaneous healing may not be possible where a belief has been imbedded in the soul's subconscious records for eons and has strong emotional content.*

*On a personal level, remember that all other beings have the same free will you do, and it may take time to correct family or work imbalances, or to bring peace to one-on-one relationships.*

*By requesting help, however, you may be assured that if you are really WILLING TO ACCEPT THE HELP, it will come to you. But, if you say you want help, and you won't accept it, or won't do whatever changing you must for the help to be successful, you will be disappointed.*

*It is vital, first, to merge your own personality and soul and, second, to join your unified soul-personality with another's. This is immensely powerful for bringing change, bringing peace.*

*This knowing that there is a God is built into every soul—into every language and culture—whatever name it is given. All must recognize that First Creator as the giver of life.*

*YOUR PROCESS FOR A JOYFUL LIFE IS:*
1. *To know where all help and peace ultimately come from.*
2. *To know when you need help, need peace.*
3. *To ask for help when you need it.*
4. *To practice peace within yourself and then between your unified self and others.*

*Your sincere call for help, for peace, is answered immediately by us in the spiritual realms and you should feel some comfort very soon, but it takes time to rebalance many aspects of the circumstances in life.*

*The call for help, or peace, is the beginning of a process in which all the factors involved are finally brought into balance once again. While the person begins to receive healing by the presence of the angels and spiritual ones who respond to calls for help and peace, the final outcome is usually not instantaneous, although each situation is unique and must be handled accordingly.*

*Then know we are not only concerned with your individual soul growth but also with the dangerous space weaponry and nuclear armaments, for we are concerned with life on this planet. All Life. Humanity's lack of appreciation for life and its value appalls us. That is why we come now. Disregard for life is not acceptable. So this is a very serious time. Nevertheless, a quick attitude change is possible if citizens of earth rise to the occasion in a massive agreement for peace!*

*Our endeavor is to improve the quality of life. Then let all humans know that each soul's purpose has to do with that same point—the QUALITY OF LIFE. Need we say that the present quality of life on earth is extremely poor? You have only to look around the planet to discover this fact. Yet there is a new murmur of love energy growing now, and we ask you to add your commitment to feed its life. We, too, are feeding it and focusing all of heaven's purpose to assist you in your triumph.*

*So surrender the despondency caused by what you see and give up your depression based upon a hopelessness that does not serve your own soul purpose or that of the planet. We urge you to take immediate action now which will bring peace and the finest quality of life for all. Quality of life for the birds and animals and plants, for people and the air and water—for the planet itself! Let us combine our efforts to this great task now, for you can help prevent planetary suicide and change an endangered planet's fate.*

*In your dreams and quiet times ask if this is the truth for you. And ask also how your soul can help you make things*

better here.  For within all human hearts is a tiny spark of
God's light.  This can be fanned into a bright glow and the
combined glow of many hearts does, and will, make a difference.  Upon this truth you can depend.

Let this be a day of rejoicing, then, for you have the chance
to truly make peace possible for yourself and for all of life.  It
was for this you came.  Now is your golden dawn of opportunity.

It is time to complete your soul contract in full measure, in
true commitment.  It is time to model peace—to bring peace to
planet earth.

**YOU ARE NEEDED!  WILL YOU HELP???**

# C H A P T E R    V
# EARTH CHANGES MAY COME

We come back to the discussion of death.

For many people physical death seems to be the most dreaded, terrifying experience of all, and the death of even one human can seriously affect those who are left behind. If someone in school does not appear and it is learned that the classmate is dead, all of the students may experience a sense of loss and disbelief that this could happen.

"I just saw her yesterday," you might say, or "He and I were playing tennis last Tuesday."

There is shock. The message is hard to accept. The mind and emotions deny the news.

In the case of a family member's death it is a particularly painful loss because the usual experience of being together is totally disrupted now. There is pain, heartache, and grief along with the awareness that all humans die. "This could happen to me, too" may cross a person's mind. For humanity is vulnerable. Physical death constantly occurs. Rarely does a person in your western nations really understand and accept death as a part of life.

Especially if you have been angry or upset with the person who has died, even if you loved him/her, you may have difficulty in handling the guilt and pain.

If negative thoughts, words, or deeds were not resolved, they may linger to fester and create an unending pain in a person's subconscious memory. The resulting hurt, fear, guilt, anger, and similar emotions are polarized energies that can be released and brought back into balance by replacing them with forgiveness and love. All relationships between humans can be cleansed this way, and one should never end a day without bringing negative experiences back to a positive or neutralized state. Your human emotions were given you by God for *enjoyment*, not to bring pain and unhappiness. If your relationships are painful, you can change them through your *willingness*. Then if someone dies—even you—there will be only a remembrance of peace, harmony, love, and the certainty of an eternal positive bonding in Spirit.

Your earth's news media tend to focus on deaths of well-known people in their write-ups. Even these casual contacts with death momentarily remind you of the very, very vulnerable position *everyone* has while living in a body. For although your Spirit cannot be demolished, your body can be destroyed or become "unlivable." Many people realize this, yet remain bound in their pain, fears, sorrows, regrets, recriminations, and guilt in their relationships, rather than improve the thinking that creates the negativity.

If there is finally to be a state of inner peace, each human who has intimately known a deceased person must go through this whole process of emotional release, of bringing love back into focus. We hope you are willing to change, to grow and learn and thereby have a happier life and death departure.

We notice your belief that older people in their 70's and 80's have lived a long life and their death is more expected and accepted. Humans may be pained about death of the elderly, but they seem emotionally able to let go of them more easily than the young. (This is not necessarily true in circumstances where the so-called senior citizen has had direct care for children or grandchildren, however.) Your western cultures, especially, do not deal well with the death of younger people—children or teenagers. There is a feeling that they have not had the chance to live a full life—that they have been cheated somehow—that their years were snatched away unfairly. Worst of all, some might think that this was done by a vengeful God—a mean, despicable Creator. Or they may blame other persons involved in the event, so as to pin responsibility upon someone or something for this untimely event. If an automobile accident was the cause, parents may place blame on the other driver, or on the doctor if the patient died during medical treatment.

Blame is quickly assigned. A scapegoat must be found. Seldom is it assumed that the person's death was a *soul choice*, whether a single death or a group catastrophe. That way, humans can disavow any responsibility for their own death. Obviously it is God's fault or some other culprit's. Yet, we tell you, this is a belief to unlearn. Look to your own soul's contract for the meaning! In this understanding you will come to know the whole you, and you will find peace.

Now, if you multiply the personal experience of one person's death by large numbers on a ship or plane or train this concept may seem impossible. Yet consider what we have said. Then when you hear about one of these massive soul contract completions, where hundreds or even thousands of people die or get injured, you will have a more balanced perspective about it.

Realize that even in these stunning catastrophic deaths souls are not unaware of a purpose and a necessity for the transformation back to Spirit. So do not be fearful of mass death. Do not say, "Humanity is helpless; we are only a vulnerable straw in the winds of God's embrace." Ignorant ones say such things

75

and believe that it is God creating such a mammoth destructive force. But in truth it is coming from your wounded Mother Earth, hurt by the careless damage you have done to her. She is crying out for healing.

What am I suggesting to you? That, when you are helpless and hurting, you tend to blame God, but this is not appropriate. You are not the weak, helpless things you think you are. You have been careless with your power, however, and this has brought the planet and all of humanity to this critical Time of Awakening.

Now, there may be sudden and terrible changes in the earth's weather patterns, causing unusual storms, tornadoes, hurricanes, or tidal waves. If only one such event should occur, there would be an emotional release of it in a fairly short time. But if there were a continuous series of such events, leading to widespread death and destruction, it would be more difficult to understand. And the shock that would accompany this kind of death toll would be great. For most humans it would bring overwhelming anxiety, fear, and numbness.

Therefore, we would like for each of you to consider and prepare yourself to accept that, if you saw such an event or catastrophe occur, *it would NOT be caused by an angry God out to punish.* It would NOT be God doing harm to innocent people. But rather, through some soul blueprint that you cannot fathom and you dare not judge, these particular people would have decided not to live on this planet any longer. They would have arranged to leave either individually or in a large group. Please try to understand this process!

Also understand that the earth needs cleansing due to the negativity that humanity has created here. Some souls will leave before the cleansing period, some during, and some will stay to form a heaven on earth. But know that for each one it was a soul decision and was not some swoop of fate or some uncaring act of devastation by a cruel, heartless God. Each of you reading this book has a soul contract or blueprint. If you are wise, you will ask in meditation and/or remember dreams to assist you in knowing what your plan is. You will love God with all your heart and mind and will begin to understand that the Universe has its own plan for the solar system and your planet which you too must follow. As you look into the starlit sky surely you know other life exists and you are only a very small part of a great expanse of wisdom.

Please be willing, then, to surrender any limitations that you have around the topic of death and be willing to hear your inner truth. The experience that you will likely have, once this occurs, is an enormous sense of freedom from anxiety and fear. Without fear you will have trust, security, and peace. You can truly live!

If a time of earth changes or physical difficulty comes, then, God is not singling out this one and that one as being bad or having to suffer a terrible fate. Nor are certain groups marked with the necessity of a more difficult situation, unless this was part of their soul contracts. This agreement is not something over which people have been denied input and control. Be advised that all souls, prior to coming to this planet, made an arrangement about their life's journey, including death. (Though, to be sure, many of them forget it and neglect to complete the learning and growth for which they came!) Perhaps most importantly, they made agreements about the time and circumstances of their passing back into Spirit. For that is what death is! A transformation time, a "beaming up."

Therefore, if you should witness or experience some catastrophe, like an earthquake or other earth change, know that the dead and dying go back into another realm or relationship with that called the LIGHT, or GOD. *Do not judge this event, for you cannot know what another's soul choice has been.* You

77

are not wise enough since you are not in contact with the records of that soul's purpose. Please understand, it is *your own soul purpose* you should be concerned with at this time. For this is the Time of Awakening. It is a time when each soul must accept responsibility for what it has created and no one may stand in another's place. These contracts require each person to be peaceful, to love the planet and all life upon it. No one is exempt from this purpose. No one.

So, if something were to happen to others—or even to yourself—know that it is part of a story being played out upon the screen of time in which the citizens of earth are participating at the level of their commitment and devotion to God. Those who will not make such a commitment obviously cannot fulfill their contract with the ONE who created all. Be willing, then, to see your purpose clearly and to complete it joyously. Nothing else you do in this life will bring you the bliss and contentment that fulfilling your soul's contract will.

Regarding the cleansing of this planet's negativity—you can help. If many people bond together in peaceful commitment, if life is honored and preserved, then the cleansing can be eased and kept to a minimum. You normally clean your home area when it gets dirty. Now the planet must have its dirt (caused by humanity's negative thinking and behavior) cleaned and upgraded to a higher vibration. So know there is a strong possibility that changes may occur in your lifetime, depending upon the speed with which human personalities respond to their soul missions.

Much of the severity or intensity of what could occur rests in the hands of all earth dwellers, so do your best to bring peace and preservation of all life to your planet. Encourage others to do the same.

Still, it is best to be prepared for the possibility that there will be some planetary changes and to plan accordingly. That is, stay tuned into your own higher self each day in meditation and go wherever the light tells you to go or do whatever your inner truth advises. Even if the planet is to be cleansed, those connected to their higher communication source will always be guided appropriately. Just as many earthlings now listen to the daily planetary news, the light workers will receive guidance on their inner radio or TV.

*REMEMBER THIS: All who die will leave the planet in the state of mind and emotions they have created, so it is essential that this state be quiet and peaceful. Understand this for yourself and for others so you can assist them should you be called upon to do so.*

What does this mean? It means that if you should witness some so-called calamity where many people—either known or unknown to you—should die physically, you can help. For they may not know everything you know. Most importantly, do not judge the event as bad! Some of these souls may be going to a higher place of consciousness than the earth.

During any emergency stay calm and call to that higher portion of yourself which is the soul. Ask to know what you should do in any given moment. Ask to know where you should go, what you should say, and to whom you should speak. If you are asked to assist another, do it.

The best and highest thing you can do for yourself, and for those around you, is to call to the Holy Light—to God, or the Holy Spirit, or Jesus, to the angels, or to any name that represents love and safety—to guide and protect you. Should you be in some circumstance where a building is collapsing, for example, and you think you can't escape, the highest thing you can do for yourself and all those around you, is to face it with *calmness* and say, "I call upon God's help—upon the pure and Holy White Light—and ask for my highest good"—or any words to that effect with which you feel comfortable.

Ask God or your *highest* symbol of light and goodness to be with you if something seems bound to occur that could affect you and/or those around you. You are never without guidance if you request it! Even though you may not be able to see the angelic ones, or those of the vast brotherhoods of light awaiting you, be certain and be glad they are truly available should you decide to acknowledge their power.

The one thing we hope you can grasp is that, if you select a moment of peace, even under challenging or frightening circumstances, by calling to your own soul and those who guide and guard you, it will benefit you. For unless you ask, this soothing balm and wonderful support cannot be given. Cannot be given! Why? you might ask. Because this is a *free will* planet where no one can be forced to do anything, unless it is the person's choice. Earthlings may force one another to do things through torture, persuasion, bribery, or violent means, but the spiritual dimensions cannot interfere or interject unless their aid is requested. This is the law. The only exception is when lifeforms on a planet would adversely affect other life beings in adjacent areas. And it is this situation that you face now. Your human life is a danger, not only to itself but to the planet and all it contains—and to "the beyond" called space, as well.

Now, should your own time to leave the planet come, do not be afraid. Simply surrender to the experience and state that you are willing to go back to the Holy Light, or God, quietly and calmly. In this "letting go and letting God" moment, you certainly will make an easy transition to your new estate and find a warm welcome awaiting you. This transition out of your physical body into your soul level of understanding is a moment to be anticipated, because that reality is the true one. Earth reality is like a movie theater or TV program filled with illusions and phantoms created by your minds. This is your world, not God's. At death's calling merely allow whatever needs to happen and do so in a gentle and peaceful manner. Inside yourself, trust the God forces, even though the external events seem like gargantuan despairs and tragedies.

You can assist others to understand this, also, for many holy books speak of this ability to just flow with whatever experience comes.

Do not be emotionally attached to your body and all your earthly possessions, for when you appear to be separated from them you will have enormous pain.

The greatest gift and the kindest, most loving, thing you can give to someone who is possibly dying, is a prayer. (Naturally you will assist in whatever way you can to give physical treatment and relieve pain.) Then say out loud to the person "Be at peace. Be at peace. Ask for the Holy Light, or God."

Please listen with your heart and know that *death is not an extinguishing of life*. It is not death really, but rebirth. Even if you do not understand it all, just surrender to that which occurs in peace and certainty. Help others do the same. Should it be necessary, state the words which we have shared, or any other prayer or meaningful saying, and help other persons attain their peace, also. It is a generous and caring thing to do at the time of another's death. Then know, if you are in such a position to help another, it is clearly for a reason and follow your intuition, guidance, or inner-God direction in any such occasion.

There will never be a soul living on this planet who will not be guided and cared for *if they ask for it*. Let us repeat that statement so you will always remember it. *There will never be a soul on this planet earth who will not be assisted at death and guided into the Holy Light if that is their wish.* You have only to speak! Call on God or Jesus, any saint or favorite spiritual leader or teacher of any time or place—any source which

81

comforts you. Whatever name or language you are speaking will be heard.

Simply say, "Even if I do not understand what is happening, I accept it and ask to be taken forward to God, into the pure and Holy White Light, into my highest good"—or whatever statement you wish.

You can call to the pure and Holy Light at any time, any place, under any and all circumstances. Begin using it today. Just ask for the Holy Light to guide and protect you. By establishing that commitment through your free will choice, you join an immense group of souls whose allegiance to God has brought forth many universes and lifeforms. You have only to ask to receive this power and love in your life, as a first step.

This is the Time of Awakening. Then accept the knowing you are forever Holy Light and cannot die. Death brings a continuing opportunity to live and know God more abundantly.

Now let us resume the discussion with you about the probable coming earth changes to remove any concerns you possibly have about what may happen and why.

Most of what may happen would be caused by humanity and its mistreatment of the planet and its lifeforms. Some of humanity's actions are more dangerous than others. We absolutely discourage any underground testing of nuclear and hydrogen weapons and armaments. *Hydrogen is a vital element of this Universe!* Anything that humanity does *in* the earth or *to* the earth has repercussions in other places. This is pure science—and the result of such damage and harmful energy in one place has to be released someplace else. Because much of the testing of nuclear—and now hydrogen—armaments has been going on for years (your time), only part of the pent up reaction has been released through earthquakes and movements of the earth's plates, tremors, volcanic eruptions, and weather changes.

In areas where underground explosions have occurred, spiritual forces have endeavored to balance the inner pressure; however, this has not been entirely successful. The underground testing that is still going on, and will go on unless you stop it, also comes from areas unknown to you, such as Mongolia and Afghanistan. You see, Russia and the United States are not the only countries contributing to global underground physical tensions by their testing programs.

Understand that these underground tensions travel very rapidly around the entire planet. These tensions and vibrations are impulses of energy, forces that move under, along, around, and across the meridians seeking weakened places to be released. Even those seemingly remote regions, when one looks at a map of "civilized" areas, *are not really remote from each other*. **You truly are one earth!**

In addition to underground vibrations one should consider the consequences of an event like the Russian nuclear discharge in Chernobyl, only on a larger scale. Yes, people must consider the possibilities of malfunctions in nuclear plants. Many times the operational failures are not considered dangerous until they happen. (This type of accidental malfunction would be in addition to deliberate acts of war.)

One must realize, then, that there are many locations upon the planet where various unknown underground testing plans are being executed. Many nations are involved and there is little, if any, publicity informing the general public even in so-called democratic countries. These things are usually very *secretive*! Considering the consequences from either accidental or deliberate atomic or nuclear power explosions, whether on the planet's surface or in the atmosphere, it should be clear that action must be taken to prevent these. WAR and the threat of war must end.

83

The forces of light cannot assist in the *prevention* of nuclear malfunctions or manmade explosions, which could bring about tidal waves and serious earthquakes in areas thousands of miles away from the regions where the accidents or acts of aggression occur.

Nor can we prevent foolish actions of cutting down trees and causing soil erosion, thoughtless pollution of air and water, or damage to animal and plants worldwide. These are *human errors* which affect many places on the planet and which we cannot control. If you ruin your water supply all life will die. There is no substitute for water and, likewise, what will you breathe if your air is ruined?

So stop your atomic and nuclear likelihoods of war, revere life and save your planetary environment immediately. Also prepare for climatic earth changes which might come and involve the entire planet. These could include every type of so-called natural happening or catastrophe already mentioned. Prepare for extreme weather patterns, tornadoes, hurricanes, windstorms, sandstorms, snowstorms, dry spells, torrential rain, flooding, and erosion—for the PROBABILITY of these activities is high. These are the effects of man-caused abuses to the planet; they are not God-caused. They reflect the efforts of the planet to heal herself. We are assessing the thoughtless, deliberate violence you have done to the planet, but can not truthfully guarantee what may happen, or when, because your military experiments are still going on!! How long will you allow these things to continue?

These imbalances you have caused in one place throw other things out of balance elsewhere. So a time you might call Armageddon or Tribulation or Reckoning lies ahead. THIS WILL NOT BE ALL AT ONE TIME OR RIGHT AWAY. But what will start to occur are unusual weather patterns throughout the world.

84

In America, the things which would normally occur weather-wise will be worse than usual. Some disturbances, not usually associated with a particular section of the country, may very well happen, such as tornadoes where before there were none, or earthquakes where they wouldn't be expected, or windstorms in usually non-windy areas. The things that usually happen will be longer and more severe and there will be many weather surprises.

The probable designated time for a thorough cleansing via these earth changes is a full five to seven years. It is likely that these events will permanently change certain earth patterns of climate and weather. However, since there is no time in our world, we cannot be absolutely precise in time estimations for your dimension. But you must be alert.

The weather intensification will likely start in the fall of 1986, so that by February and March of 1987 there will be a severe winter season. In the spring or end of April, 1987, there may be unusual rain, windstorms and floods. It is possible that sandstorms and windstorms will occur throughout the western region of the United States along with dry spells in California, Arizona, and the Texas area.

The winds and snow in the mountainous regions—Rocky Mountains and Sierra Nevada—are likely to be more serious or severe than in many years. There will be trucks and automobiles stranded in the mountains, for instance. Travelers, take your precautions! Be prepared for these probabilities, but not fearful.

IT IS NOT THE PURPOSE OF THESE THINGS TO CAUSE DEATH.

The purpose is to heal the planet. Still, it should also help humans to be aware of their mutual dependency—to teach that, regardless of other real or imagined differences, they need each other as humans. It doesn't matter which state or country people live in, all are part of humanity. When a challenging event happens all tend to work together for the common good. IT SHOULD NOT TAKE THIS TYPE OF EVENT TO BE-COME ONE FAMILY! BUT WE NOTICE AN EVENT SUCH AS A TRAGEDY OR CATASTROPHE OR DISAS-TER MAKES PEOPLE REALIZE THEY NEED EACH OTHER—THAT THEY CAN BE FRIENDS.

Why should it take something severe before people see one another as friends? Does it really take some tragic event before they call for help, extend aid, and trust one another? If the an-swer to this is "yes" or "maybe," then some experiences in earth changes offer an opportunity for humanity's growth to-ward compassion and caring. Indeed, it was and is the hope of the spiritual powers that such events would not be necessary.

All of humanity had in its early beginnings the opportunity to learn about caring for life. This is still the goal each soul is to achieve here on planet earth! God does not seek to destroy any life on the planet. God does not want to take human life or wish things to get difficult.

What you are to strive for is compatibility, friendship, and an expression of caring—or what you call lovingness towards other lifeforms whether human, animal, or plant. You are to seek <u>PEACE</u>!

Now these things which have great probability of occurring, *unless humanity moves into peacefulness quickly,* will involve changes not only in the earth, but will have a domino effect or chain reaction, as well.

When land is affected food will become scarce. The ani-mals will have to seek other places to live and many of them may die for lack of food and water. Your water will be af-fected which is one of *the* most important things on your planet.

You require fresh water. Every single form of existence needs this liquid. And the purer the water is, without chemicals or pollution added to it, the healthier the existence it provides for plants, animals, and human life. The entire circle of existence is healthier.

The same is true for air which must also be pure, not polluted, and the same remarks are offered about it.

Earthquakes in metropolitan areas will create the greatest demonstration of people needing people, but they may also show the greed and destructiveness of humans even in times of tragedy. Lawlessness and looting by a certain portion of the population are common even now after such events. Your governments should plan for such probable emergencies in case they occur.

Fortunately, you have organizations and groups which come to the rescue of humanity during its times of trials and tribulations such as fires, floods, and epidemics! And these humans provide an orderly example of commitment, service, and caring. They use measures or procedures and teamwork which the rest of you should also exemplify. Every human will have opportunities to learn from earth changes at both the soul and personality levels.

We hope that many networking communities will be established *prior* to these coming events so that their knowledge can assist in the process of planning for comfort and survival. These changes should be thought about *before* the probable disasters begin, and your preparations should begin consciously with careful planning!

With all of these things occurring many people will start to ask, "Who is causing all of this? Is this God's will?"

That is the big question of this time.

People are going to meetings and seminars and lectures where the topic of earth changes is the focus and they ask, "What will happen to me? Will I be safe?"

Most of them go away from those meetings and take no action, even if they are given information about survival and the most likely safe places to be. They change none of their habits or patterns of behavior to align with prophesied data and accept no responsibility for implementing the information. It wouldn't even have to get to a cleansing if people would behave in a peaceful way all around the globe.

Why is there no understanding until an event actually happens to people and they have to learn the hard way? Can humans not understand compassion until they need compassion shown to them directly because they are suffering?

Action NOW is the critical factor. This will alleviate the possibility of despair. Plan ahead and be fully prepared for the possible events, praying that they not come.

THESE EVENTS ARE NOT PREORDAINED BUT ARE PROBABILITIES. We have noted that some humans place truth in a prophesy, but then take no actions of their own to turn it around by a change in their behavior.

A prophesy is the likelihood or probability of a certain sequence of events and circumstances occurring. There are two kinds of prophecies: first, the reward offering kind, an urging toward achievement; second, a warning of what will happen if you don't change negative behavior. A wise human being would, upon reading this information, change his/her behavior to live up to the recommendations of either or both types of prophesy and the principle behind it. For the principle upon which this planet was created, and life brought to it, was: Harmonious living and existence of all lifeforms—peaceful relationships, so that there is no destructive tendency or urge to harm any other lifeform. It was expected that even for food, an animal lifeform would *not* have to be murdered. From the beginning the plants were designated as food for both mankind and animals.

Through the probable disaster period and this cleansing time there are adjustments that will happen. **There will also be signs and wonders from heaven that will be a part of the earth changes.** Does that sound too good to be true?

Yes, there will be at least THREE major events during this time, which will bring the awareness of God into your personal experience on earth—which will bring about a more rapid awakening! These events will strengthen those who already love and revere God and hopefully will bring multitudes back into the certainty that they have a true relationship with the Creator, also.

The populace will have visions of events that will truly awaken the human heart to the certainty that God exists. With this change of heart it is hoped that the entire planet will awaken and return to its primary purpose for being. Earthlings are a family, living together in a home which has many levels or rooms. But it is still one place and one family, even with its divisions or apparent separation.

Then determine to have peace on planet earth! And to care for all the life that is here. This is your earth focus and purpose. Haven't there been enough wars and cruelties from the gassings and trench warfare of World War I to the atomic bombings of Hiroshima and the present Star War weapons. Do not allow the possibility of a nuclear, or other, holocaust to be developed further with the *horrible*, unconscionable weapons which some of your minds have created. How could any creation of God envision such destruction? This insidious thought process must stop if the planet is to be saved.

Now, we say to you young people, *you* must turn the tide of this murderous thinking wherever you can. The institutions which carry forth such ideas must be deterred; there must be action taken to eliminate negativity from the souls of mankind. It is obvious to the most casual observer that violence fills too many minds, as well it might, in view of the past millions of years dedicated to that pursuit. But it was not always this way for earthlings. No, quite the opposite. There was a time when life was peaceful. There was a time when, as a group of beings, you cooperated. There was a time when you thought that caring was very important, and all life upon the planet was under your keeping. Yes, every single lifeform is yours to protect, to communicate with in a kind way. We will speak no more of this, except to point out that you have an opportunity to change the course of destiny—the destiny of humanity on planet earth. By the power of your belief and the certainty in your heart, peace is possible and must prevail. You can turn the tide on those whose beliefs have become frozen and locked into negativity.

It is very important, right away, to take responsibility for the condition the world is in and to begin at once to link with others like yourself whose intentions are peaceful. See now in your mind's eye a joyful, gentle, peace-filled world. A world where, on meeting one another, there is an immense bonding, a spiritual caring that takes place. This love bonding holds and cements relationships with the mortar of peace and acceptance, regardless of the color, sex, creed, or nationality of the separate individuals.

Yes, we are concerned for life on the planet, deeply concerned. And it is that concern that brings us to you to give you this information, so very different from that which you will read in your usual school textbooks. It is not that the authors are deliberately trying to keep the truth from you; many simply do not know. But ignorance is a limitation which will continue until enough of you take responsibility to change it, which we hope will be very soon. It is because earth's humanity is so filled with this hatred and bitterness and strife and war and bloodshed that we come in remembrance of who and what you really are. Indeed, you are peace, which is light, which is joy and caring. This is the hallmark of the New Age. This is your credential, your pattern of being in the world.

In days of yore, millions and millions of years back, a God-spark was placed in you. That spark within you still yearns to be released in peace and love, still glows deep within you. Sometimes it is buried and covered over by the human personality, so much so that it has no identity. But the truth is you are a creation of God! And deep inside, you know this to be true. You know it! And it is time now to accept that. This is your identity. You are needed in the world to change the flow of those negative thoughtforms and activities into something positive. This is the job that each soul on the planet has at this time: to revere God and to care for one another. It is time to create a positive reality! Then sudden calamities caused by earth's radically altered health—its weather patterns or even the movement of the earth itself—will not frighten you. For you will truly know your soul purpose in this Time of Awakening.

You are the purveyors of peace; you are the wings of pure light who carry the truth and who will, with a deep intention of the heart, assist the planet to rise upward in glory.

Let there be no more men on battlefields, or in various war machines, in misery calling for mercy in God's name, or in the name of Jesus, Mother Mary, or other saviors and great teachers. For their cries and screams are recorded in your subconscious memories. The terror, the anxiety, the fright—it is all a pattern of horrible suffering. But it is time to eradicate all that pain; time to free it and let it go. It is time to change in very real and obvious ways. So let us agree that, no matter how terrible earth's past experiences have been, no matter how extraordinary the measures are that we have to take in order to change that condition for the better, pain and suffering must end. Therefore, we will send healing and cleansing energies to you and the planet during this year.

Know that humankind has always struggled with the elements, with the animals, and, mostly, with the personality self in relation to others. These same aspects exist in society now, but this time all of heaven seeks to bring you forth in peace! We gladly bring help and caring to all who wish to accept it.

This Time of Awakening especially requires cooperative interaction, but also solitude and close association with God through prayer and meditation. It is that time when you must bring your personal energy of light to share with others in group meditation at least once a week.

Every individual needs to find personal truth in this Time of Awakening and bring it into group action. Let each individual agree s/he doesn't want a government which kills, or plans to kill, other humans—or any other life. Let a groundswell of peaceful intention influence government to return to its true purpose on the planet—which is PEACE. Cooperative caring is essential!

Stop war! Bring it to a halt once and for all time. Be willing to step forward and establish a new world, a New Age—a golden dawn of radiance.

The Time of Awakening is here. Nothing on earth can stop it. And after it, if it becomes necessary, comes the Time of Reckoning. In the end there will be a magnificent radiance on earth, at last. Yes, a Time of Radiance comes.

Make your choice wisely with heartfelt determination and soul focus. Be counted on by those of us in the Divine realms to play the part for which you came. Peacemaker. *Caretaker of the Earth.* Perhaps the letters "C.E." should be the initials you place after your earthly names to show the specialization, or spiritual desire, you have? *Be an expert in caring.* Be Mary Smith, <u>C.E.</u> or John Miller, <u>C.E.</u>.

Discuss these things with your own inner being and let the light guide you along every path of confusion, through every moment of darkness. For the light is God-given and connected to a power so immense you can scarcely comprehend its nature. Even our words in this publication must be substantiated by your own soul knowing, however, as you learn to be the light which shines with truth's bright glow.

Then peace be yours, offspring of a great and noble parent. Another time we shall speak of your God connection as your avenue for survival in this time of probable difficulties.

# CHAPTER VI
# FROM SURVIVAL TO RADIANCE

When an animal senses danger it takes action to protect itself; humans seek safety, or physical survival, in a similar way. Yet for humans the only true survival skill lies beyond the human body and is *spiritual* in nature. A love of God—in or out of the body—is the only thing which assures soul survival anywhere in a Holy Light Universe. This reverence for God is the basis or foundation of life. It, and it alone, is the connecting link between your soul and your personality self. Without this connection to God a soul would know great pain!

However, in speaking just of physical body survival, humans can be aware of a potential emergency and they can use this awareness to take necessary precautions before the event occurs, while animals don't possess that foresight. Preparation is the demonstration of your awareness!

This *awareness*, to be followed by *preparation*, is available to nearly all humans, but it remains to be seen whether our information will be taken seriously and acted upon by you and all of humankind. We hope you will pray and meditate daily in order to have the inner guidance and connection to direct you through the possible dangers that lie ahead.

Since the only survival skill you can count on is trust in God and in the mighty realms of light that are a part of God's helping team at this time, use it! "Tune in" each day, through inner quietude or meditation, because it will be a frightening world in the coming years without God's security. Who but this omnipotent source and its creations can broadcast helpful information or advice to you on the planet? Who else knows the path and soul contract of each human being on earth?

Yes, you will want this cosmic advice and support to steer you through a world of probable turmoil. Then use prayer, contemplation, and meditation as the tools to contact the God force, and be consistent in these practices. A navigator is needed for *every* plane flight. Don't attempt life without your own communication and navigational support!

Now be it known that each young adult is expected to begin meditating in a very regular fashion. For the first *four months* of your meditation you must meditate 15 to 20 minutes at least three or four times per week. After that four months period you are to increase the frequency of your meditation to nearly every day, and finally to a *daily* meditation time. In addition, be certain that you join with others *each week* in a group meditation time. This may be with your family and older adults or with your peers, PROVIDED A SERIOUS INTENTION IS PARAMOUNT AND MAINTAINED. Socializing after the meditation is proper. During the quiet you are all to focus only on God, however. It is recommended that you read New Teachings for an Awakening Humanity for a more complete explanation about the purpose and ways of meditation, or you may consult other sources you feel drawn to as a method of quieting your mind and listening to God.

Violence is so much a part of humanity's nature that it gives rise to many of your terrible problems. Yet we would prepare and guide and protect all beings who wish to be peaceful. We ask for a spark of your willingness to revere God and assist the planet and all life upon it. We request that you accept our support and caring during these years of so-called tribulation.

The <u>New Teachings for an Awakening Humanity</u> book has already called forth a Love Corps, a group of those who, regardless of religious or spiritual memberships or beliefs, have a love for God in common. This is a group of souls that has gone beyond its former understandings and has joined a vast groundswell demanding peace. We expect others, coming from all walks of life, to join as well; we expect their hearts to answer God's soul call. They live in a variety of climates and nations, in the mountains and by the oceans. They reside in deserts and by the riverlands. And everywhere their numbers will swell and grow. For this is the Time of Awakening planned by us in the heavenly realms. This is your hour of response to God's soul call.

Because violence is so much a part of humanity's nature at this time, we would suggest that much psychospiritual cleansing needs to be achieved by all human beings upon the planet. You are required to accept responsibility for your thoughts, feelings, and actions. It is recommended that you delve into your character to see what you can improve and how you can grow in emotional stability and balance.

God has given humans their emotions, but they must learn to balance them and not run amuck under sudden stress. In the past your selfish beliefs and strong personality distortions have created havoc all around the planet—and now threaten space. This will not be allowed in the future, so you must bring the personality under the direction of your soul and its God-connections.

This self-examination will serve you well during difficult times if you have sorted out some of your attachments to ideas, things, and people. This will be valuable to you when changes begin to happen very quickly, for you will have already freed yourself of personality wishes that tie you to old ways of thinking and behaving. Spirit is ever-expanding. Personality is ever acquiring, limiting, judging, and controlling. Be willing to learn how your personality operates and how it dominates or manipulates others in order to have what it values. And remember that any undesirable line of conduct can be changed. You can become very aware of your thoughts and in noticing them you can detach yourself from the personality's whims and motives which have not brought peace to planet earth over the eons of time.

Now is the clean-up phase introduced by the Time of Awakening, necessitated by humanity's unlimited personality rampage spanning millions of years. By coming to know yourself and learning new behaviors you can do your part of the self-cleansing which all of humanity must accomplish. For all of these individual thoughts and feelings and actions of the past have compacted and become like a gigantic cesspool overflow that must be cleaned up. As the New Teachings for an Awakening Humanity book says about the planet, "You have soiled your home."

Survival, then, depends upon your awareness that you are more than your body and that the higher part of self can override and redirect the follies of your personality.

Even if you have been struggling with your personality's demolition tactics, you can have the great awareness that will help you survive. *You can ask for help.* By this single action do you open the way for guidance and assistance to come to you. This requires willingness—willingness to acknowledge God, willingness to free yourself from the personality's domination, and willingness to ask for help from both earthly and divine assistants.

Emotional cleansing is a major survival issue in everyone's life, then. Even in everyday life upon the planet it is wise and healthful to sort out emotions and feelings on a daily basis and to come to a state of completion, forgiveness, and balance with them. This not only establishes a peacefulness in the mind and emotions which can be reflected into the body, but it releases an individual from the control of these negative energy patterns. Such patterns rob you of a centered and focused expression of spiritual truth and behavior.

No one upon the planet has an absolutely perfected human personality, though some come very close. Fortunately, absolute perfection is not required. It is required, however, that you desire to keep the emotions in balance! and, should they slip into negativity, that you get them back on center as quickly as possible. This is not always easy to do when humans have held onto such different ideas about life, about God, and about their earth activities. Still, it is possible to work toward compatibility and not to fall into the childish habits of destructiveness. Humans must strive towards a peaceful balance point, so they can avoid murder, war, and the extreme positions of hatred and control that lead to devastation.

Avarice and greed, as well as personal power in political, financial, and social matters, have long been the hallmark of earth gone astray. This is a result of the fact that most people are not centered on their highest point of reference with God. For no one who earnestly respects and carries forth God's true principles can desire subversive solutions. The two do not go hand in hand.

The question for earth today, more earnestly sought now than ever, is: will its inhabitants follow the principles given as guidance by the Creator of life?

The present situation on earth is not a pretty picture. Yet *you* can bring hope and change through your knowing and your actions at this critical time. There have always been individuals who remember God and the purpose of earth life. They have forever been the ones who bring surcease and healing. But at this time there will be more than a few; there will be a large group of light bearers working together all around the globe. You can choose to be one of that helpful number which will grow in size during these next months of spiritual awakening.

Yet we must speak of the greatest barrier all humans face in times of crises. That barrier is fear, including panic and other negative emotional outbursts. Yes, more so than many of God's other lifeforms, you of earth have the opportunity of pure emotional panic. Therefore, we suggest training periods where these topics of survival are put into practice and people are sufficiently informed to act intelligently under stressful conditions.

Take care of this preparation from a point of clarity, not fear. Prepare and organize your own household and join your neighbors and community in a unified plan of commonsense response. You came to achieve spiritual mastery and you need a body to help you do that. Then proceed with that genuine understanding and sense of security, because you can be guided and protected in life if you choose to be. So can all other souls. Then choose to have guidance and security and let us begin our teaching and learning venture together.

Preparation always alleviates the tendency toward panic; and people will become more stable when trained for emergencies. They will have a plan of action to follow and this will preclude chaotic and foolish behavior. Being prepared for emergencies, then, moderates fear and anxiety and creates a state of emotional comfort and security.

You already have wonderful youth and adult organizations of many kinds which can be useful in these matters, as well as an array of published books and pamphlets to read or study.

We only briefly outline here some obvious major survival considerations which your publications discuss.

The foremost survival need your body has is *breath*. Your body needs clean, pure *air* from which to absorb oxygen into the lungs. You have heard that a body can suffocate in a matter of minutes, and this is so. Consequently, keep earth's air as clean and pure as possible. Toxins and radiation in the air must be kept to a minimum for the body to maintain itself. Work arduously to avoid air pollution caused by agricultural, industrial, governmental, or military pursuits. Any pollution is not in the public interest because it travels widely and spoils the atmosphere for all. Air is critical, not only for human survival on the planet, but for all other lifeforms here, as well.

Next comes water. Water is more critical even than food, because you can go longer without food than water. Water, like your air, is polluted by agriculture, businesses, and companies that have toxic wastes or by-products, and by your own government's disposal of atomic and nuclear wastes, just to mention a few. Even individuals contribute to water pollution through the use of pesticide sprays and a variety of recreational activities. There must be controls to prevent water pollution and frequent inspections to enforce regulations for the welfare of all. Fresh water supplies are dramatically diminishing.

Do not deny your responsibilities regarding pollution of the seas and oceans either, for many living creatures have their origins and life continuity therein. Although humans do not have permanent residence here currently, they are the Caretakers of this earth and must protect the sanctity of all life.

Obviously, in a time of weather changes and earth difficulties, you will want to have storage containers with gallons of water per person in the family—enough to last at least two weeks—and also canteens for drinking water in your vehicles. This is common sense.

In the same way, you will want to have food enough to last several weeks in case of a catastrophe of some kind. This, too, is common sense.

Other sensible preparations would include warm clothing in case of cold or freezing weather. The human body is vulnerable to sudden temperature changes and to any radical exposure to heat or cold. Ingeniously designed and organized, the body nonetheless has to function in the physical world and it must follow the rules of physical existence.

Your concerns, without becoming obsessive or frightened about them, are: air, water, food, clothing, shelter, a safe environment, and knowing enough about the human body to be able to aid others should they go into shock or be injured. First aid training is a good investment for everyone! Keep a first aid kit and related supplies handy.

Such items as waterproof containers with matches, candles, and kerosene lamps are useful. Humans do not like the cold and dark, and if the gas and lights are shut off for a considerable length of time, warmth will be needed and a light would be both practical and cheerful. (The Silver Ray created moonlight for this reason, so that even during the dark time away from the sun, there would be some light on earth to comfort you and call your soul remembrance forth.)

Authors on your planet have already written many camping and survival books which would be useful in your every day life necessities and activities on earth. Perhaps you will look at some for your edification?

Although these next years will be full of challenges and apparent obstacles, the Time of Survival will be accomplished and in its peaceful aftermath will come a wonderful period called the Time of Radiance, the Golden Age.

We have shared that, even during the time of adversity and reckoning, you will be guided individually by your own inner

102

source of help. There will also be major experiences for all earthlings which will confirm God's magnificent presence—that power and caring you cannot now see, hear, or sense. At last! At last, humans will see and sense God. In these future days, they will know, finally, that the wonderful Creator is real, is caring, and they will feel that certainty thereafter.

This Time of Radiance is the final purpose, outcome, or even the reward for going through the cleansing of earth's compacted negativity and the elimination of its potential danger to the Universe. And it is this future of radiant spiritual evolution that we wish you to keep uppermost in your mind during any possible harsh experiences in the physical body.

You are being raised to a new and wondrous future now and we assure you that the outcome will be more beautiful and glorious than we can describe. See if you can find a place of trust to hold this truth close to your heart and let its warm certainty keep you safe until you actually witness the light and feel the presence of that mighty ONE yourself.

Here, in the density of a world where consciousness has fallen into the blackness of hell for the most part, there will yet be the radiance of the Gold and Silver Rays of God. It was for this accomplishment of peace and love that you left your faraway planets and star clusters and came to this place called earth. You were determined to bring God into physical matter and never to lose your reverence and caring regardless of the cost. You did this for your own self-mastery, for the planet's spiritual advancement, and to create a future filled with a joy unspeakable.

All on earth are invited to partake in this sequence of events leading from the Time of Awakening through a Time of Tribulation, Reckoning, or Survival to that greatest experience possible—the Time of Radiance.

The time period of awakening you are in now is much like a race in which you decide to enter and see it through. That is what the Time of Awakening is all about—each one choosing God and bringing peace to the planet, whatever it takes.

Let us carry the illustration, or comparison, of the race even further. In the beginning—as a runner—you have much strength and are eager to complete the event. After several laps around the track, or after some distance on the straight-away, or up into the hills, you become weary and may consider dropping out. Yet, if you persevere through the weariness and overcome thoughts of quitting, there comes a second wind, or renewed strength, and you continue onward. Soon you see the goal ahead and are brightened by the sense of joy because you've endured this far and are close to the finish. Perhaps you imagine a trophy or the great satisfaction of crossing that finish line. For *all* who finish will gain greatly in this venture on planet earth.

So, too, as in a race, when people are in the Time of Awakening, they must have strength and vision to go through the Time of Reckoning, glimpsing always the light ahead, the promise of the God-graced goal of radiance. The great difference in this race or event is that you are not competing one soul against another, but running cooperatively as a team. And your cheering section consists of a vast armada of light beings who work with you to accomplish heaven's part.

Also, during the Time of Survival, remember that the Godhead will bring forth those three divinely spiritual experiences, previously mentioned, which will thrill and encourage humanity. Even though Spirit is presently, but temporarily, invisible it is your *essential* ingredient for human progress.

In the New Age, containing the awakening and reckoning years, it is *cooperation* that counts. It is mutual enterprise, not just individualism, one against another, that will prevail. Caring cooperation is an evolving concept for humanity to learn quickly and put into positive practice at all levels of human interaction. Governments must begin with *sharing* as a planetary theme. Those who have abundance will not let others go hungry. You will care for each other as a family of ONE heart, ONE mind.

Remember, then, that the Golden Age, or Time of Radiance, will be the greatest experience any human being can have. For there will be an absolute awareness and experience of God's presence and power. The higher forces who deliver that immense energy will also be seen and felt. And there will not be any resistance to the guidance of God, once that omnipotence and power is displayed!

This is not coercion or control we speak of but a wonderful joining and participating with all that truly is. A happiness beyond words!

*THE TIME OF AWAKENING THROUGH THE TIME OF SURVIVAL (OR RECKONING) INTO THE TIME OF RADIANCE CONSTITUTES ABOUT 25 EARTH YEARS, BUT CANNOT BE PINPOINTED PRECISELY. THERE-FORE, DO NOT ATTEMPT TO DO SO. THESE TIME SPANS ARE BEST THOUGHT OF AS PROBABILITIES.* Merely become aware that changes are on their way and begin your preparations for them in a sincere, comprehensive way, without fear, turmoil, or confusion.

The progression of earth changes and cleansing, called the Time of Survival, will be followed by *several years of great quiet and peace and then the greater radiance will commence and continue.*

To achieve this progression from Awakening to Radiance we again recommend regular meditation, both individually and in groups, as the only security an earth resident has in the years ahead. That is why we have come to guide your awareness, encourage meditation, and give our support.

Some will choose doubt and fear, but you will not, because you will be gliding along a path of non-selfishness. Only the selfish doubt their origin and thereby choose fear. Doubt is a *mental* condition and fear an *emotional* response to it. Those who follow their ideal path with God are fearless and courageous, for what can be lost in the wholeness of light and certainty?

All religions advise that fear is the root of humanity's troubles and that perfect—or unconditional—love casts out all fear. That is, love overcomes mental doubt and frees the personality's emotions from uncertainties and worries. With such an understanding fear has no foothold or room to grow, and peace will dwell gently in your heart and mind.

You may have had fears in the past. Let them be acknowledged and released. Perhaps you have feared what others would say about you, feared that you would not be liked, would be judged and found unworthy. Recognize such fears and let them go. Most of all, acknowledge any fears of the unknown that you may have, especially fears of a future filled with change. Face it and work with releasing fears that stem from material things which have no eternal reality. Work until you can bid them goodbye. Remember that the Light has not willed for any soul to suffer or want or worry. Trust this greater certainty and truth and you will develop as a well-balanced personality completing your soul's contract with God.

As you model faith and trust, many people will be eased and comforted by your presence. Seeing *your certainty* they may wish to know how you have dismissed fear from your existence. During stressful times it is this very healing presence which brings God to man.

Then focus on the Light and let the darkness fade from the reality of earth. *You* are a new seed born to bear perfumed blossoms of love and peace in every rainbow color. Is this not a blessing you would accept rather than the pain and folly of fear? Is this not a blessing you would teach an endangered humanity?

Now, one of the greatest gifts to be extended to humans during these years leading to the Time of Radiance is improved mental aptitude. As you must know, only a small portion of the human brain is presently used, even by the greatest human geniuses who have lived. But now that is to be changed and most everyone will have improved intellectual acuity or greater "brain power." This is needed to avoid the continuing problem of having very few humans of genius caliber, some of whom invent things or create activities not in the public interest. When the time comes that most people have the capacity to think deeply about ideas and to work together for their highest and best use, society will change. But with this intellectual advancement a heart desire for peace must also be indwelling or humanity will get into deeper difficulties and continue the misapplications and miscreations of ideas for weaponry and war.

You have already seen a great increase in human intellectual capacity during the past 47 years. This will continue; however, it must have the caring and concern for all life added to it or you will yet destroy yourselves. Then vow this day to love God and to bring peace to all life upon this planet. To do less is to have an even harsher learning lesson ahead.

Along with this increasing intellectual advancement must be established the *human values!* Without this balance humanity could perish. The human values must undergird the technological progression, and this you have not yet managed to do. It is urgent that this occur. Please hear and acknowledge this need and take action to implement it at once.

It is our desire that humanity survive its past collective neg-ativity and learn through its God-given emotions that caring and love are paramount virtues. The planet will be healed. And so will those of you who seek it. You stand on the brink of an immense mutual regeneration and evolution of your planet. Don't miss this exciting chance to become self-mas-ters! And also members of an advancing super-conscious cre-ation.

This time is one of increased openness, so you may freely begin discussions with your peers and other adults about the problems humanity has brought to the planet and what can be done to solve these difficulties. For, as these awakening ener-gies come to earth from Divine sources, more people will want to be involved in such matters. There will be an interest in holistic health—in cleanliness of self and the entire planet as a whole body—in the relationship of a pure environment—and in developing cooperation between all lifeforms which constitute planetary life. Perhaps the coming earth changes will foster a greater concern for the oneness of all life than you presently have? Since this "wake up!" time is intended to increase con-cern for the preservation of all life and a consistent state of peace, this would be a logical outcome of that theme.

Then STAND IN READINESS. This is your watchword for these coming years. Be certain you do whatever is required to provide caring for your physical vehicle but do not worship it. In this time of return to God, while still living in the density of form and matter, it serves a vital learning opportunity.

Most of all, however, recognize that your spiritual survival is assured. There is no death! Even if you see the death of one or many, it is only their bodies they have laid aside for a greater reality. For those who can persist in the body, there will be a monumental moment of enlightenment as your third-dimensional planet is raised up into the lighter density or dimension where creation begins.

Those who prepare for survival under God's protection will enjoy life doing whatever their inner guidance leads them to do on a daily basis, certain that all is well. Even now, please know you are cared for in ways that your word "love" can't convey, and know also that one day you will experience that caring first hand.

What will it be like, this new radiant earth?

It will be so unique that your earth words cannot do it justice. You attend many different kinds of events upon your planet now, but no one has ever seen the spectacles that await you, of this you can be sure. The three experiences of God will be world changing events!

In this upcoming, radiant time, existence will be harmonious. All lifeforms of mineral, plant, animal, and human will be cooperating with each other. There will be a complete absence of destructiveness in nature and human relationships, resulting in a blissful existence.

The quality of life will increase as peace reigns at the focal point for all that occurs. Truly, the human spirit will soar to the highest level possible while still living in a physical body, and creativity will peak higher than ever.

You will still have free will about everything except violence and negative actions. Harmfulness in thought will end, and caring will take its place. Count upon this change for that is why the Time of Awakening, followed by the Time of Survival, and then the Time of Radiance, is here. This is a certainty, for it is *God's* proclamation!

This Golden Age, this radiant return to peace, is not something any person of goodwill would want to miss for, just as your holy books have said, much will be revealed then that cannot be known or told now. Still, humanity inches toward that great change with every breath of caring, with every thought of God, with every moment of love demonstrated.

The earth, herself, will sparkle in a new sundance of lighted splendor which will further increase with the negativity removed. And you will have soulfelt gratitude that you have lived to see this great time no matter the effort it took. You will, then, be eternally grateful that your soul commanded your attention today and led you to remember and choose God while in your three-dimensional body.

This God-choice is required of all who would know the Time of Radiance, the time of genuine and long-lasting peace. Relax, then, into the truth of your inner confirmation and let the glowing recollection of its promise brighten this upcoming flow of change, movement, and growth. Know that the future is bright and after the winter's storm your earth home will once again be bathed in God's light upon this precious garden which was created with such intense, loving care.

An increasing radiance of the Gold and Silver Rays, or the power and caring of God, is even now glittering around the earth but most cannot see or feel it yet. Trust, however, that the time grows closer and closer when that sun/moon radiance will gleam in the air like a spring shower of dancing rainbows, and prepare for the touch of its presence upon your soul with an ecstasy known only in the higher realms.

You are about to be enclosed in the touch of universal energy and light. You will soon have the prize you sought over eight million years ago, before humanity came upon the face of the planet. You will have held steadfast as Caretakers of the earth and completed the goal of peace and love set by God for this creation and this family of lifeforms through the darkest of experiences into the sunbrightness of peace.

Truly, this is the climax of promises made and promises kept. In your lifetime, youthful ones, the return of the prodigal sons and daughters will be achieved.

Graduation comes soon. Be sure you are present, Creations of Light, Creations of Love.

Peace be yours eternally.

AMEN.

# A D D E N D U M
# MESSAGE FROM THE CHRIST

I shall speak to you in modern language, unveiled by other people's interpretation of me, so there will be no confusion about my message or its true purpose. The simple teachings quoted from my life as that one called Jesus still have validity but so much has happened in nearly 2,000 years that these teachings must be updated and put into your present world perspective. My message of peace, love, and forgiveness still has the same basis but your technological advancements into space weaponry and underground explosions of hydrogen and nuclear materials has changed the situation drastically. Now I must come! sent by the very One called Parent-of-us-all. Earthlings may not create any planetary disaster which would effect the fabric of space which is a great womb of light and energy, constantly birthing new life and maintaining all of the Great One's prior creations. It is a gigantic life supply which must not be ruined or damaged.

Although there is a small percentage of truly peaceful beings living on your planet, most humans are unawakened and have forgotten their God connection. They have spurned the warm invitation of the many spiritual teachers and angelic essences to assist your return to the conscious awareness of your true identity as a creation of wisdom and beauty. A creation, beloveds, without malice or will to do harm to self or others!

As your present world teacher I do not come alone. Over five million volunteer energies work together on your behalf at this critical time. We are a team—a rescue team, if you wish. We seek to change your present path of horror before it is too late.

Unaware, and deprived of the Divine fourth dimension, you sleep in the darkness of unremembered identity. You suffer a nightmare which must end. A few of your leaders seek peace but most yearn for personal power and control in the name of defense, in the name of safety from others who would harm them. See beyond this lie, for they commit a spiritually criminal act by their constant attention to war, violence, and disunity of the human spirit.

Out in what you would call space, the great planets, star clusters, and other energies you do not presently understand, planet earth has been labelled with one word: *criminal*. Therefore, God decrees that any actions of your military experimenters and governmental supporters for war must cease. Violence must end and war be seen no more. We do not wish you to be sucked into another's misuse of power where only self-annihilation waits. Surely you know of what I speak in your hearts' deepest certainty.

Where are the gallant, pure souls dedicated to peace and the preservation of all life on your planet and beyond? Where are those noble ones dedicated to turn the tide of violence and war to gentleness and caring? Where are the souls of lofty belief who promised to save a dying, endangered planet? It is likely that you are one of these or you would not be reading this book, so know that you are not alone in your mission and that we are here to help.

You may ask how humanity can turn the tide toward peace in a short time—you may say the task is too overwhelming to accomplish. But I tell you that the challenge is not impossible for a loving heart and a willing mind. Not in this time of nearly instant manifestation which accompanies the immense energy we now pour upon the planet. Perhaps if we were not sending you these great amounts of light, energy, and love the challenge would be impossible. But you are not alone in your opportunities. You are being transfused with cellular healings of love and light. Energy from us is in the air and all around the planet. Take advantage of it and use it to manifest what you would have regarding peace on the planet.

The positive intention, or daily affirmation of love—the simple belief and agreement that earth shall have peace—is your basic tool to use. Then accept what we offer in the way of support in this time of great manifestation, so that the purpose of your little wills can be served by those of us who love you and carry the responsibility to see that the plan works out on earth.

For there is a plan and you are its followers whether you know it or not. And the plan has its culmination time very soon. To aid you in making its completion a successful one we of higher consciousness are serving you with increased energies and immense amounts of light. Therefore, your own personal lives and those of your world brotherhood and sisterhood are greatly empowered to reach the fourth dimension of consciousness.

In your life on earth all of you have tasks of one kind or another, and all of you have skills and various interests which you pursue with great intensity and purpose. In this time of humanity's evolution I ask you all to make peace and the preservation of all life your greatest desire. Make it your <u>number one</u>

priority. For it can be done when such attention and willingness are given to the Divine plan.

Give yourself wholeheartedly to this effort, beloved ones, so all of humanity will be freed of its negative limitations, and the family of man will go forth boldly in the great love effort required at this time. We notice that you talk, walk, or march for peace, but I say to you that if you do not join in a mutual meditation with us during these activities you lose much of the healing energy.

Please provide us an avenue through which our energies may join yours. At any meeting, but especially in those with high attendance, you should always ask God to join you in energizing prayers or images of peace for the earth herself and all upon her. Then MEET and MEDITATE! Ask for all human hearts to become peaceful and to relinquish violence and separation. Let earth become unified in peace once again.

No peace organization with only a survival-of-self motive serves the greater good of all humanity. And if it does not call to the heavens for blessing and assistance it is weak indeed. We notice that many peace organizations are afraid to use the word "God" for fear many people will not be drawn to their efforts. In this we are not allowed to interfere due to your free will. But peace is a spiritual issue, if you think about it, and your peace organizations' attempts to bring change by adding additional numbers only works if the intention is based upon the power of love in your hearts. Since love is God, there is no avoiding such a connection. Therefore, if the leaders of the various peace movements fail to recognize the source of peace as love and the source of love as God you will lose great power in the movement. Combine them all with the mortar of commitment, however, and your results will be phenomenal.

Recently we noticed meetings of peace groups in which not a single meditative or contemplative thought was used to bring

the separate energies of the people together.   NOT ONE.
Therefore, because the audience had not focused its tremen-
dous energies into a single channel of intention, much power
was lost.

Let it be known, then, that the purpose of your own designs
cannot win without God.  Hasn't your past history taught you
that your own efforts have brought war and violence—less than
the desired effect?  Do you really believe that humanity, without God, can surmount the horrendous effects of your past errors?

No.  And this is not said to discourage you.

It is said to remind you that your own plans, without the
guidance of God, have failed you for seven million years.
Surely it is time to acknowledge that the assistance of your
Creator is needed.

I hear comments among the peace leaders saying that "if we
get religious we will lose our members."  I say that if the members among you refuse to acknowledge God, you foster a sickly
purpose indeed and there is no cure for the diseased state in
which you dwell!!!  For it was your self-chosen motives and
separation from the Great One that caused your fall in the first
place.  Do you really think in your feeble attempt to make it
better that you can do it all by yourselves?

I say it again.  Your peace movement will fail without the
recognition of a power greater than yourself which YOU
MUST INVITE into your midst.  No, we do not care what you
call it.  Call it God, or use phrases such as Source, Creator,
Power of the Universe ... Holy Light ... Holy Energy ... and
so on.  But the invitation must be offered in order to have the
additional light and energy given.  At a recent meeting of thousands of people who were hoping to change the course of humanity's disaster, not a single mention was made on your TV

117

about calling forth the higher power. Hear me a final time: **This does not serve your cause at all**.

What does aid and assist it is to acknowledge that peace is love and love comes from the Creator. Therefore, invite the greater presence to be there with you for we can imbue each person with greater awareness and with the sense of peace within, which will assist in creating peace on the external level of manifestation.

You are image makers given free will. You image frequently but without sufficient intentions for peace. Your thoughts must desire peace and your hearts must also long for it if this negative separation is to cease.

Let me ask you a few simple questions. If you were fighting a fire and had only 30 firefighters while the fire had already blazed so far out of control that the whole countryside was on the verge of destruction, would you insist on standing there alone or would you call for an immense armada of airships, men and materials that would be helpful to you? Or if a plague were discovered in a certain town or region, would members of the small, local medical staff call upon outside help or would they merely attempt to handle the situation by themselves?

In these questions and your answers I hope you see the message I bring you. The God-of-All has said we are to give you immense energy of love and peace in these troubled times ... and we await your call. We who would work with you cannot do so unless you request our help—unless you express a willingness to call out for assistance.

We stand ready, in ways you cannot even imagine, to give you our energy and love to help you in your many tasks and works in the months ahead.

If you fail to include the aid of higher consciousness, your efforts will fail and you will bear the effects of a personality-induced purpose. For if humanity fails to understand that your yearning for peace is a response to the call of God to the human heart to love, you misunderstand the entire history of humanity's soul evolution. This would be ignorance at its highest! It would signal yet another defeat in mankind's eight million year adventure on earth. Without God you are cruel, at best. Without God your heart is empty of love. Without love you could die as individuals, nations, and as a planetary citizenship.

Therefore, even if you only call upon the nature of love to give a cohesiveness of purpose to your peace meditations, meetings, marches, and other activities, I suggest in the very strongest of terms that you do this. MEET and MEDITATE. Begin by stilling the group, gathering, or audience and then focus all minds and hearts on the nobility of love. Agree to express only the best of humanity's God-created nature. For in that agreement you center the most powerful holy energy in the Universe as your assistant. Ask always for the pure and holy light forces of the Universe to come forth to assist your cause and to aid the work. To do less than this is to allow the fire to burn uncontrolled and the plague to spread unchallenged.

Do you hear and understand my concern? Will you accept the offer of our higher, peaceful realities to guide your worthiest mission?

In the name of our Creator I ask you to accept the strengthening assistance we stand ready to give. Know that we await your response through soul willingness and personality behavior change.

You are the seed of a new humanity. You are the tomorrow of love trembling to be born. You are a cosmic being in the making. Acknowledge this as your true identity and join with all of heaven's power and caring to complete the task at hand.

The planet and all of humanity need your aid in establishing peace on earth. We must move quickly, in strength and certainty, to reclaim this planet for the Light.

Time is critical. Will you help?

In peace, and always with a greater love than you have found, but eternally seek, I call you forth to your glorious hour.

AMEN.

\* \* \* \* \* \* \* \* \* \* \* \*

## *Love Corps Networking*

Creating peace on our planet requires commitment and co-operation. If your soul has been touched or your life goals clarified by this book, perhaps you would like to share its message with friends and acquaintances ... give copies for gifts ... write letters to the editors of newspapers, magazines, etc. about peace ... seek peace publicity on radio and TV stations ... have a fundraising event to support such endeavors ... form a local Love Corps group to meditate weekly ... generally help raise humanity's consciousness about the preservation of all life on earth. The Love Corps is an alliance of all human beings who want planetary peace above all else and will work with others to achieve it.

The vital thing for each of us is to meditate daily and also in a weekly group so that we will always have God's presence guiding our daily lives. If you are new to meditation and need temporary support while developing your own inner guidance, we have been asked by The Christ energy to provide a monthly newsletter. It will include answers to reader-submitted questions about the book's concepts and will give any critical messages needed by Love Corps volunteers of all ages during the Time of Awakening.

A Love Corps team will be traveling around the United States to link energies, to share additional information not included in the New Teachings and Secret Truths books and to encourage humanity's achievement of peace and the preservation of all life upon planet earth. If you would like to be involved in the Love Corps endeavors, to participate with us in classes, have individual soul readings, or receive our support, please write to us so we can include your area in our itinerary.

\* \* \* \* \* \* \* \* \* \* \* \*

# *Participation Questionnaire and Order Blank*

To:    SPIRITUAL EDUCATION ENDEAVORS (S.E.E)\*
        1556 Halford Avenue, #288
        Santa Clara, CA 95051 U.S.A

Having read <u>Secret Truths for Teens & Twenties</u>, I want to participate in spreading its message. The way I choose to do this is indicated below.

I wish to donate my skills and/or time for:

| | |
|---|---|
| \_\_\_ Secretarial/clerical support | \_\_\_ Fundraising |
| \_\_\_ Bookkeeping &/or accounting | \_\_\_ Publicity |
| \_\_\_ Graphic arts design | \_\_\_ Public speaking |
| \_\_\_ Word processing | \_\_\_ Other |

I have the following equipment:

\_\_\_ CB radio         \_\_\_ Ham radio equipment
\_\_\_ Personal computer: Make/model_____
I (am)(am not) qualified to operate the equipment checked above.

Please send information on how I can help disseminate <u>Secret Truths</u> to:

\_\_\_ Friends, bookstores, churches, and organizations
\_\_\_ Other countries (foreign shipping rates will be
      provided)

I would like to help publicize <u>Secret Truths</u>:

\_\_\_ On radio \_\_\_ On TV \_\_\_ In newspapers/magazines
\_\_\_ Other (specify) _____

I would like to be a networker or contact person for the Love Corps in my area. \_\_\_

(Continued on reverse)

Please send me the monthly Love Corps Newsletter:

_____ A 12-month subscription for <u>1987</u> is $30.  $_____
\- or -
_____ Single issues @ $3 each - circle month(s):
J F M A M J J A S O N D          $_____
_____ The 9 back issues for <u>1986</u> (April-Dec.) for
$24 or $3 each - circle month(s) desired:
A M J J A S O N D          $_____

_____ I would like to help you pay off the printing of <u>Secret Truths</u>.  (For tax-deductible contribution, make check payable to The Share Foundation*)          $_____

Please send me additional copies of <u>Secret Truths</u>:

Quantity _____ @ $7.95 per copy          $_____

I wish to order _____ copies of <u>New Teachings for an Awakening Humanity</u> @ $8.95 per copy          $_____

Minus discount if applicable (see below)**          $_____
Plus 6.5% sales tax (for CA residents only)          $_____
Plus shipping for 1 book (in U.S. only)***          $___1.60___
Plus $.70 shipping for each additional book          $_____
Total for books (U.S. currency only)          $_____

TOTAL ENCLOSED          $_____

*Please print:*

Name _____

Address _____

City/State/ZIP _____

Phone (optional) (_____)_____

*S.E.E. is a project of The Share Foundation (Fed. EIN 94-2699567)
**Love Corps volume discounts:
5 - 9 books @ 10% off plus shipping
10 or more books @ 20% off plus shipping
***Please request foreign shipping rates.